"They call me Fred..."

the LANDLORD

by Fred Miller

TRUE AND FUNNY STORY ABOUT LIFE AS A LANDLORD

I dedicate this book to my parents,
who raised a great kid,
and to Bev and Sam, who give me a reason to live

Special thanks to Deb, Jackie and Paul for their thoughts
and
Bev, who puts up with me
('cause there's more to come)
and
Steve Milroy for his fabulous cartoons and cover
and
Bob Ashforth and Glen Peers who really did a terrific job
working with my "beer and pizza" style of writing

Warning!

This is not a How-To-Do-It book.
It's more of a How-I-Did-It book.
The author makes no promises or guarantees, explicit or implied, about how this book may alter the unfolding of your life. Many of the experiences described in this book should not be attempted at home, and parental/spousal guidance is strongly advised.

F.M.

Contents

Chapter 1	In the Beginning	11
Chapter 2	Banks	15
Chapter 3	Now What?	16
Chapter 4	Hello, Mrs. Real Estate Agent	17
Chapter 5	The Hunt is On	19
Chapter 6	Me... Negotiate?	23
Chapter 7	Lawyers	25
Chapter 8	Moving Day	27
Chapter 9	First Impressions	29
Chapter 10	Rent Day	31
Chapter 11	Life's Not Good!	33
Chapter 12	Patience	34
Chapter 13	Important Things	35
Chapter 14	The Handyman Strikes Back	37
Chapter 15	The City Strikes Back	41
Chapter 16	BBQ Season	43
Chapter 17	Rules of the House	45
Chapter 18	Sprinkler System	47
Chapter 19	Revenue Canada	49
Chapter 20	Project Planning Time	51
Chapter 21	Project Implementation Time	53
Chapter 22	Project Construction	57
Chapter 23	Loose Ends	61
Chapter 24	The Years Go By	63
Chapter 25	Strange Feeling	65
Chapter 26	The Twilight Zone	67
Chapter 27	Teach Me, O Great One	69
Chapter 28	My Bro	70

Chapter 29	The Hunt Is On... Again	73
Chapter 30	Strategy Time	75
Chapter 31	Caution, Construction Zone	76
Chapter 32	My Learning Curve	79
Chapter 33	Things Happen!	81
Chapter 34	Tenants	85
Chapter 35	Arbitration: Tenants 1, Landlord 0	86
Chapter 36	Appliances	89
Chapter 37	Life's Problems	92
Chapter 38	Arbitration: Tenants 2, Landlord 0	93
Chapter 39	The Smoke Alarm Works Fine	95
Chapter 40	Toilets	96
Chapter 41	It Happened So Fast	98
Chapter 42	Simply Amazing	101
Chapter 43	Sinks	107
Chapter 44	Things Are Still Happening!	108
Chapter 45	Driveway	111
Chapter 46	Illegal Suite? Not Me!	113
Chapter 47	Garbage	115
Chapter 48	Rock Walls and Balconies	117
Chapter 49	A Fateful Day	120
Chapter 50	Here, Kitty, Kitty	123
Chapter 51	Doggone It	125
Chapter 52	Arbitration: Tenants 3, Landlord 0	126
Chapter 53	Handyman... Yeah, right	127
Chapter 54	Arbitration: Tenants 4, Landlord 0	129
Chapter 55	Paint	131
Chapter 56	Moving On	132
Chapter 57	Rent Me!	135
Chapter 58	Father's Day	139
Chapter 59	My First Workshop	141
Chapter 60	Golf	144

Chapter 61	Workshop Maneuvers	146
Chapter 62	Exercise	149
Chapter 63	Real Estate	151
Chapter 64	Income Tax Maneuvers	152
Chapter 65	Inside Looking Out	155
Chapter 66	Fred's Brewery	158
Chapter 67	Basketball, Insurance and RIP	159
Chapter 68	Mind Set	161
Chapter 69	Just Another Day	163
Chapter 70	Dust Bunnies	167
Chapter 71	Philosophies	170
Chapter 72	Reward System vs. Bonus System	175
Chapter 73	Intensity	176
Chapter 74	The Magic of Cooking	179
Chapter 75	Send in the Substitute Landlord	183
Chapter 76	Another Day, Another Life	187
Chapter 77	It's Raining	191
Chapter 78	Reference Checks	194
Chapter 79	Attitude	196
Chapter 80	Landlord School	201
Chapter 81	They're Back	205
Chapter 82	Video Game	207
Chapter 83	Fetch, Good Boy!	213
Chapter 84	Tenant Conversations	215
Chapter 85	What I'm Really Thinking	219
Chapter 86	Tenant Teasing	221
Chapter 87	Things To Do List	223
Chapter 88	The Path to Free Money	227
Chapter 89	Wacko Land	230
Chapter 90	Moving On... Again	234
Chapter 91	Sold	237
Chapter 92	Send in Substitute Landlord #2	241

Chapter 93	Another Day... Again	243
Chapter 94	Tenant Rental Application Form	246
Chapter 95	Application to be a Landlord	250
Chapter 96	True or False	252
Chapter 97	Deep Thoughts	255
Chapter 98	Fred's Gumbo Soup	257
Chapter 99	Salmon and Soul Searching	261
Chapter 100	Going, Going, Gone	267
Chapter 101	Impossible	269
Chapter 102	Going, Going, Gone... Again	271
Chapter 103	The Tenants' Secret Handbook... Unplugged	274
Chapter 104	To Whom it May Concern	280
Chapter 105	Twenty-one of the Most Guarded Secrets of Landlords	283
Chapter 106	Life's Good Again	286
Chapter 107	The Conclusion of the Matter	289
Attention!		292

They call me Fred...
the Landlord

Chapter 1

In the Beginning

I was thirty-three years old and still single. The football season had just started. Life was good. On this particular Sunday morning, I was surveying the pizza boxes from last night's party in the hopes of finding breakfast. The only thing I could find were two slices from a vegetarian pizza. "That's the last time I let a girl order the pizza," I thought.

I was looking forward to a full day of beer, pizza and football. Dozens of people would be in and out of my place all day, watching the game on TV or throwing the pigskin around during halftime. Not necessarily outdoors, either. Didn't matter. Some people have their houses child-proof; mine was football-proof.

Sometimes girls came over to watch the game. They always looked interested in watching the game, but I noticed as they got married to my football buddies they **both** stopped watching football games immediately after the honeymoon. Most of the time I never saw them again. I think there's a hidden message in the wedding vows between that "sickness and health" bit and the "richer or poorer" thing. Somewhere in there the groom is getting sacked instead of the quarterback.

Anyway, I was eating my vegetarian pizza and reading the newspaper. I had my standard allotted time to spend: twenty-five minutes reading and five minutes getting cleaned up before everyone got here. They never knocked when they came in, so you had to be careful when you got out of the shower. No one was ever invited over. They just showed up!

I still remember reading the article in the paper like it was yesterday. I couldn't believe it, but they were canceling the Registered Home Ownership Plan. I had been putting my $1,000 into this plan religiously every year for the last eight years.

How could they do this to me? I had a long-term plan (my only one), and in about twenty years I would have saved up enough to buy a house. I figured by then I would know all about electrical things and plumbing stuff, and I would save bundles of money because I'd do it all myself. I wasn't ready to buy a house. I didn't even own a screwdriver!

The article said I had one year to put my money towards a house or it would be taxed. I wasn't an accountant, but I knew that being taxed was not a good thing. For eight years I'd been getting my little tax refund because of my long-term planning skills and great vision. And right there before my very eyes my vision was about to be taxed. I had one year to come up with a new long-term plan.

The obvious solution to avoiding the tax was to buy a house. I could borrow somewhere around $80,000 at fourteen percent to avoid the tax. The tax, in reality, would have been around $2,000, but the point of the matter was that it was **my** $2,000. If I had to pay bundles of money to a bank for a mortgage, well, that wasn't the same thing. I'd blame that on the new plan and the newspaper article. My old plan had been perfectly good for eight years and shouldn't be subject to the tax, and that was pretty much it.

You see, up until that point everything had been fine. I had three vehicles: a motorcycle, a van and a car. All three were insured, just in case I wanted to use all of them on a particular day. My other assets included $300 worth of furniture. My bookcase made from boards and bricks probably had the highest value, next to the TV. There was beer in the fridge and canned goods in the cupboards, and that pretty much made up my total financial worth. I didn't include all the gas and oil in my vehicles, but I knew it was there.

My bank account had a permanent $1.00 balance and was used strictly for cashing cheques. Any interest on the account was cleared out annually. I didn't know it at the time but my life, as I knew it, was over. I turn forty-five next month. Here's what happened during the last twelve years.

Oh yeah, they call me Fred.

Chapter 2

Banks

So, the first step. I went to the bank to get money for the house I wanted to buy. I hadn't found a house yet, nor had I even looked, but I knew if I found one I'd need money. I didn't expect any kind of a problem, as I had accumulated $8,000 and I'd been a loyal customer for eight years. I had even paid them to get those cheques printed. You know, the ones with the scenic picture in the background. I had a whole box of them that had never been used. The address on the cheques was from an apartment I had rented a very long time ago but I figured, since the apartment was still there, the cheques should still be good. That is, if I ever decided to use one and the cheque was for less than a buck.

I was expecting, well, not so much the royal treatment when I got to the bank, but at least a lot of respect for my savings and a well-executed eight-year plan. I expected the owner of the bank, or at least the next guy in line, would want to ask me questions about things like commitment and long-term vision, which I obviously had eight years of experience in.

The actual interview *per se* only lasted about a minute. I wasn't sure, but I think they had the wrong file. There were only two pieces of paper in it and I recognized one of them, but I thought for sure it would be a lot thicker after eight years.

I found myself standing outside the bank, not really sure what had just happened. It was August and hot outside. I remember I wanted a beer, and I wanted my own house. I could only have one of them, and the pub had air conditioning.

Chapter 3

Now What?

"Never say die" was not **my** motto. It was someone else's. I started to plan what I was going to do with my money from the Home Ownership Plan. I thought about buying a new mattress for my bed; the kind where everyone doesn't roll down into the center of it. It was impossible to fall out of my bed.

But somehow, although I don't know the intricacies of the brain, I knew mine was working on something I had never authorized. Somehow I knew there was more to this, and I had every right as a man to get out there and get a second opinion. The very next day I found myself outside a different bank (and then a different pub). I was going to teach my brain for humiliating me (again).

I think the main problem was that I didn't understand how banks work. I was at the basic hunter/gatherer level when it came to understanding the banking system. I knew you had to sign papers if you wanted to borrow money, and I figured you just had to sign a lot more papers if it was a lot more money.

I started to look for books on banking. I figured the obvious title to the book I needed was "How Banks Work." Well, it didn't take long to find out that banks don't want you to know how they work. There was a banking system, all right, but it was top secret.

I needed professional help. Someone who was willing to help me through this. Someone to take my dreams and my investment, and make things happen. I needed a Real Estate Agent!

Chapter 4

Hello, Mrs. Real Estate Agent

I didn't actually know what a real estate agent **did**. My parents had always done the talking when I was at home. But I figured the title pretty much said it all. So through a friend of a friend of an acquaintance, I found someone who came highly recommended. We set up a meeting and she immediately started to collect my personal data. That's when I realized my vision of the kind of house I wanted contained a lot of "I don't know" and "I don't care." She called me flexible.

It didn't take long before she realized I didn't have much money. She said it was a big challenge, but she'd accept it as she was still looking for her first sale in real estate. We were a perfect match: neither of us really knew what we were doing.

She brought out the Multiple Listings in real estate. It was like ten phone books pressed together in one. She said I could look at the book, but I couldn't take it with me. I told her the shocks in my car couldn't handle it anyway.

We started to talk and get to know each other over lunch. For the first time in a long while, I wasn't sitting in a pub by myself wondering what just happened. She paid for lunch. Things were picking up. I felt bad, but she said it was a business expense and she could write it off. "Against what?" I wondered. We had identified a number of houses I wanted to look at in several areas that were suitable. I couldn't afford any of them.

About an hour later I started to skip over the houses that were on the waterfront, and anything that had the word "mansion", "estate" or "luxury" in the description. Apparently anything with a "view" or a "pool" was out as well. Pretty soon I realized that if the house even had the word "feature" in it, I was in trouble. There were over a gazillion houses for sale, and it didn't look like I was about to move into any of them!

I was still really interested in the house-buying process, so I thought I would get a little more insight by asking her some questions. "What was it like when you bought your first house?" I asked.

"Oh, I'm just renting an apartment. I've never owned a house."

"Well, have you ever been involved with the purchase of a house?"

"No, not yet," she replied.

"Would you recognize a house being sold if you saw one?"

Oh well, she bought me lunch, so I might as well give her a shot at it.

Later, she did a purge of all the listings that I couldn't afford. We made a date with destiny, and set off to all three properties that made it into my price range. She asked if I was good with tools, because they were all "handyman specials." I told her about my other dream of owning a Robertson screwdriver and knowing how to operate it.

We had a good laugh, but by then my brain had started to hurt.

Chapter 5
The Hunt is On

The next day, I viewed my first house as a potential home owner. I didn't want to tell the real home owners that it was my first time. I felt like a virgin. I thought I had better ask questions that were insightful and meaningful to the process.

"Where's the bathroom light switch?" I asked.

"This is your first time, isn't it?" they replied.

I wanted to hide in the closet (if I knew where it was; I wasn't going to ask). I remember seeing these ripples on the ceiling in the kitchen. The ceiling was so low I could reach up and touch it. I ended up poking my finger through the ceiling!

"Can't be good," I thought.

The data sheet on the house showed Property Taxes. They were more than I would have lost if I simply took my money out of the Home Ownership Plan and ran. The oil furnace didn't work, but if I bought the place I wouldn't have had enough money for oil anyway, so it didn't matter. Anyway, I wanted to find a place that didn't have to pay that Property Tax thing. Tax was bad, and I wanted to avoid it if at all possible.

After the first tour I couldn't wait to see the other two places; I figured it couldn't get any worse. The Real Estate Agent told me to brace myself because "it goes downhill from here." I hoped she was talking about the grade of the street.

The next place was owned by cats. In every room. The carpet corners, I'm sure, were curled up from the cat smell, because my nose was starting to do the same thing. I really couldn't see the place because my eyes were starting to water. I like cats, but five per room should be the max. All the paint was peeling off the walls about one foot above carpet level. I realized it was kitty bum height.

There was a lesson for me to learn here but, in hindsight, I now realize it flew right over my head. I would revisit the situation again in my life, and I would pay the price then.

The last house on the list was an up-and-down duplex. One family up and one family down. If the owner lived in one suite, they could "rent" out the other suite and collect "revenue." I understood the rent part, having done that all my adult life. The revenue concept fascinated me. This would be money I would get every month to buy beer, nachos and the other two food groups. For a minute I thought that was maybe a little too easy, but then I wondered, "What could go wrong?" My brain started to hurt again.

When I saw that Property Taxes were applicable to this place, I realized there was a pattern happening here. Obviously, I was looking in the wrong part of town. As for the house itself, the grass hadn't been cut anytime this century. The roof leaked. The stove and fridge were so old that I couldn't tell which was which. I figured I could put a beer in each one of them and see which one came out cold and which one came out hot.

The good news was the backyard was fenced in; the bad news was the fence was so old it was falling over. The only things holding the fence up were these beautiful vines with white flowers that completely covered it. I figured the owners had put a lot of time and money into that. I found out it was called Morning Glory. Beautiful name.

Inside and out needed paint. I had never painted before, but it didn't look like a big job. One good weekend would do it, I figured. This was the third place I'd viewed. I was feeling like a seasoned veteran. If I had a Robertson screwdriver in my hand I could take this place on. I felt good about this place. Or maybe I felt so bad about the other two that this was my brain doing the overtime thing again.

I decided I wanted this place. Having only three to choose from in my price range made it easy to come up with the decision. I asked the Real Estate lady when she thought I could move in. She mentioned that some other things had to be settled first, so I told her to take care of them and I'd go home and start packing.

She laughed and thought that was pretty cute, but there's nothing cute about packing, I can tell you.

Chapter 6

Me... Negotiate?

Having decided on a home to buy, I was told it was time to negotiate. I had never negotiated anything in the past. I had always paid full price. But I learned that an "asking" price is very different from the "real" price, which I was told I would have to guess at, with the possibility of being off by thousands of dollars. Why couldn't they just tell me what they "really" would take, and I would tell them what I "really" could afford?

But no, we had to play the game properly, so how about I give you $80,000 for your place instead of that $89,900 you're asking? I was told $80,000 was too "round" a number; please pick another number. So I kept adding dollars on to my original number until $80,900 looked better. It sure cost me a lot of money to make my first number look "better." My Real Estate Agent was pleased with my progress so far. In my thirty-three years on this planet, I had never spent this much money, and I was about to sign it away in one afternoon.

I wanted to negotiate a lawn mower into this deal, but the owners didn't have one, which explained why the grass had never been cut before. I wanted to negotiate repairing the leak in the roof (it had the same feature as the first house I saw where, if you poked your finger in the ceiling, you got an instant skylight) but, because it was a flat roof, it was "common, and that's just the way it is." So as quick as my offer went in, it came back signed as approved, with a big thank-you note from the owners. I thought it was awfully decent of them to care that much.

Now all I had to do was convince a bank to give me $72,900. I wasn't walking into this with a lot of confidence after my last two banking adventures. Much to my surprise, though, this time I spent a lot more time in the bank. I still got turned down, but at least I got a chance to get comfortable in my chair before I had to leave.

Well, we then had to tell the owners I wasn't worthy of the banks. They were extremely disappointed and assured me that they would do everything they could to get my name on the title. I was overwhelmed by their thoughtfulness.

The next thing I knew I was involved in a Vendor Take back Mortgage, commonly referred to as a VTM. This meant that the owners of the house would lend me money to buy their place. Again, I was overwhelmed by their generosity. When the bank found out that they didn't have to risk as much money as originally proposed, they too were happy. They said that all that was needed now was for them to do a "routine" inspection of the property. I told them to make sure they checked out the cool fireplace in the living room.

Well, not only did I get a bill for $200 for the "inspection," but the place failed. I never asked them to write a book on the place, but there it was. There were tons of red circles and arrows highlighting the features. They said the building inspector had gone home with a headache. I asked where my money for the property was because I wanted to move in soon.

A few days later the owners convinced the bank that all the problems were "cosmetic," and that they would increase **their** VTM! The building inspector hadn't returned to work yet and his wife said he wasn't taking any calls. The bank asked me if I was a handyman, and was I just trying to fix it up and flip the property for a profit?

That was it. Time to get out the Robertson screwdriver.

Chapter 7

Lawyers

They told me I needed a lawyer. I didn't want a lawyer. When I found out how much a lawyer cost, I knew for sure I didn't want a lawyer. I got a lawyer. We didn't like each other from the start.

He showed me that my house was registered with the city. That piece of information cost me $150. I already knew the flippin' place was registered. How did he think it got there in the first place? He said he checked for "liens" on the property. I told him the flippin' building inspector had already checked to see if it leaned. Cost me another $50 anyway. I had to pay $180 for "miscellaneous disbursements." Excuse me, how does your vocabulary get away with miscellaneous equaling $180? Do you know how much miscellaneous I could get with $180 (miscellaneous beer and pizza, that is)? A whole flippin' party, that's what.

I signed my name so many times that day I developed a new signature. I gave up asking questions after about thirty documents. There was so much paperwork it felt like I was buying the entire city. I really hated this!

"Do you understand these documents in their full entirety?" the lawyer asked. He had that smug look on his face that makes you want to smack him clear across the continent. "Yes," I said, with my *I'll get even with you* tone. "I have a photographic memory." I just failed to mention that I hadn't put any film in yet.

"That will be $950, please. Cash or cheque?"

I wrote him a cheque.

Chapter 8

Moving Day

What a thrill — moving into my own place! I bribed my friends with pizza and beer to help move all my assets. Really, I just needed two people to drive my other vehicles over there while I loaded up the van. But everyone knew I got my damage deposit back from the house I was renting, so they knew there would be lots of beer and pizza.

Only one box was dropped as far as I knew. Naturally, it contained a boat in a bottle that my brother Ken had made for me. It broke open and really just didn't have the same effect afterwards. Luckily, I had packed the one plate I owned in a different box. It was the only other glass thing I owned. I didn't have a cup or anything like that, because I had learned to drink beer from the can.

When you only own one plate, knife and fork, the dishes never pile up. People always commented on how clean my kitchen was. You learn to adapt. I always bought the mini cereal packages so you could pour milk right into the box, consume, toss it out, and no dishes. For eggs, just crack a couple onto the plate and put them in the oven at 450° for about ten minutes. For hard-boiled, just put them in the sink and run the hot water over them for a while. Canned goods were easy, because they could be opened and heated up on the one stove element that worked. No muss, no fuss.

The barbecue was still a useful tool for cooking food. I had some stones that were stacked to resemble a little circle in the backyard. I used fallen branches from the neighbor's trees for fuel. I'd only BBQ when my neighbor was not around. That way I could borrow the grill from his BBQ to place on top of my stones. Steak and corn was my specialty. I'd just leave the corn right on the cob and keep turning it until most of the green casing fell off. I was mighty proud of my steaks, because when they were done I had a little bit of blue rare on the inside, followed by medium, encased by well-done. I never had to ask anyone how they wanted their steak done, because somewhere on the steak I had done it just right.

My new place had this really cool Acorn fireplace right in the middle of the living room. It made you feel like you were in a small ski resort. It would not only provide me with heat for the winter, but it was essential to the disposal of pizza boxes. Being single, I found this was a real babe magnet.

Anyway, when all the beer and pizza was gone, so were my moving friends. It took me about fifteen minutes to unpack everything and put it all away. With the ship in the bottle gone, the assets were down to around $280. I tried to burn the pizza boxes in my new fireplace. I singed all the hair on my arm while reaching in to open the flue. Most of the smoke was gone by the next morning, but there was a BBQ smell to the new place, which was okay with me.

Those orange shag carpets really pick up the scents, don't they?

Chapter 9

First Impressions

I found out that those Robertson screwdrivers come in different sizes. I had ordered a medium one, hoping that it would be the most common one. They asked me if I wanted a Phillips. I didn't know what a Phillips was, so I assumed I wouldn't need one.

My bed didn't survive the move. One leg collapsed, and the holes in the headboard were now too big for the screws to fit into. My screwdriver couldn't fix it; I felt like taking it back, but I had a great spot on my belt to hook it onto, and I looked really cool walking around with it on. With the bed gone, my net assets now dropped down to $250.

Later on, when I went to sit down, the screwdriver jammed into my thigh, ripping my pants and making me bleed all over the place. Up until then I hadn't even used the stupid thing except to stab myself with. It cost me $25 to get my bed hauled away. I explained to them that there had to be a "use" for the parts. It couldn't possibly all be garbage. They wouldn't listen to me, so I wrote them a cheque.

I looked at all that Morning Glory on my fence. I swore it had doubled its size since I had last seen it. The tenants were probably fertilizing it. I thought the tenants must have a dog. There was this path you could see in their yard that went all the way into the back. All the grass was dead in that area of the yard. The Morning Glory must have been hardy, because it was doing just fine.

I couldn't get into the backyard as the gate was stuck. I hoped that my Robertson screwdriver and I could fix the problem, but I didn't know quite what the problem was. The Morning Glory did seem to have quite a grip on the gate, but I didn't want to tear it away in case I damaged the plant. I managed to climb over the fence, but when I landed in the tall grass I stepped on an old bicycle wheel rim and twisted my ankle. Stupid screwdriver went right through my Band-Aid and ruined another pair of pants. I was going to hook the stupid thing to the other side of my belt from then on.

It now looked as though I would have to relax and let my ankle get better. Would probably help the gashes in my leg, too. Forgot I didn't have a bed, though. I thought maybe I might find a lawn mower in that tall grass, although I wasn't too anxious to go back in there right away to look for one.

Oh yeah, the lawyer called me that day and said he wanted to see me. I think it was about the cheque I wrote.

Chapter 10

Rent Day

It was time to collect my $450 rent. I thought I would get it quickly before I went out so I would have some spending money. I had already spent most of my cash on screwdrivers, Band-Aids and tape for my ankle.

I thought I heard my tenants downstairs but, when I rang the doorbell, nobody answered. I thought I'd just peek in the window to see if anyone was home. The grass in the front yard was taller than the stuff in the back. I waded cautiously along in the grass until suddenly I felt a sharp jab in my big toe. I had stubbed it on something. When I moved the grass away to see what it was, I found my old bed. How the heck had it gotten there?

Over the next few days, every time I knocked on their door, no one answered. I didn't even know what these people looked like, but their rent was five days overdue and that was all that really mattered. All my canned goods were gone. I went down again, but before I knocked on the door I found myself trying to haul the bed out of the grass. Can you believe that Morning Glory attaches itself to *everything*. That bed wasn't going anywhere.

While I was bending down in the tall grass, I heard the front door open. When I stood up to look, I saw the back of someone's head. I just stood there. I heard him say, "Come on, honey, the coast is clear." There was no question it was a bright and clear day all right, so I yelled out, "Hello, what a great day!" Sure looked like I surprised him. Well, he could only see half of me in the tall grass.

Very nice people. He explained that he didn't know I was the new owner, so that's why he hadn't given me a cheque. So next thing you know, he wrote me a cheque for the full amount. That's right: 450 smackers to carry me through for the rest of the month. I noticed that he had those scenic-type cheques like I have. Noticed the address was different, but he changed it and initialed the change. I was off to buy a new bed and charge up some groceries.

Life was good.

Chapter 11
Life's Not Good!

I couldn't believe the cheque bounced. That was my money and I wanted it that minute. Lucky no one was home when I knocked on the tenants' door, because I was furious. The furniture shop called and they wanted their bed back, or a new cheque and $20 for the bounced one I wrote. I told them to talk to my lawyer.

As luck would have it, I was in the front yard when my tenants opened their front door again. I was just sitting there on an old chair I found. I figured this chair was worth about $5, so my net assets had just increased to $255. Looked like I surprised them again. When I went over to talk to them, something held my leg back. It was that darn Morning Glory! It had circled around my leg. I gently twirled it off, making sure not to step on the leaves.

My tenants were so apologetic. He had written the cheque on the wrong account. They said they had knocked on my door numerous times trying to give me a new cheque in its place. I told them it was an honest mistake and just to forget about it. Unfortunately, they had just run out of the proper cheques, but there were new ones on the way and they would be here any day now. If only I had been home when they had looked for me.

So I wasn't getting any money, but what I was getting were letters from my bank wondering where my mortgage payment was, and letters from my lawyer talking about legal action. The utility companies weren't exactly friendly with their little reminders, either. About the only solution I had was to drink all the remaining beers in the fridge and get the deposit back on the bottles.

Chapter 12
Patience

Well, I was into my second month as the owner of my new domain. I felt sorry for all the problems my tenants had run into with their bank. They still had not received their new cheques in the mail.

To compensate, they let me use their portable BBQ. I had some friends over and I filled the thing up with briquets and got ready to do my famous steak and corn dish. While we were preparing potatoes inside, I heard a loud knock on my porch door. When I went to see who was there, I saw my neighbor pointing at my sundeck, which was on fire. The bottom of the BBQ was so rusted, all the briquets had fallen out and started my deck on fire. I mean, it's not like I wasn't thinking of replacing the old deck, it's just that I wasn't planning on it right away.

We got the fire out and I returned the BBQ to my tenants. They were a little upset that I had damaged the bottom of it. As for the balcony, it seemed to be fine structurally. I think all the Morning Glory around the railings was keeping everything together. The fire didn't seem to bother the plant either.

It was the first time I had noticed Morning Glory on the second floor.

Chapter 13
Important Things

I started to learn important things:
- Robertson screwdrivers not only come in different sizes, but they are also color-coded.
- You need more than one screwdriver.
- Everyone is capable of writing a bad cheque — the tip-off is to watch for the scenic background on the cheque.
- Morning Glory is actually a noxious weed, and I had a lot of it. Plus, the root system travels to the center of the Earth. It attaches itself to *everything*.
- Water is not free — you get a water bill.
- Banks don't like you missing mortgage payments, no matter how good your excuse is.
- Buy your own BBQ.
- When your brain starts to hurt, listen to it — it's telling you something.
- Guests resent having to bring their own plates, knives and forks.
- Carrying a Robertson screwdriver on the left side of your belt will cause exactly the same amount of damage to your leg as carrying it on the right side.
- Don't bother displaying a boat in a bottle when the bottle's broken off. Too many questions from people.
- Tenants have a secret handbook containing excuses for Landlords.

Chapter 14

The Handyman Strikes Back

Okay, I'm a man and I was available for work, or handy, so to speak. Technically, that brought me into the "handyman" series. There was work to be done, and my fees were lower than anyone else's. I was free.

The art of borrowing tools was essential to my success. The barter system has thrived for years, so I thought I'd give it a try. One of my neighbors, who I sort of knew, had just finished cutting his lawn. I went over to the fence and offered him a cold beer. He was very appreciative. I told him I was caught between projects because I didn't have the right tools. When he asked me what I was doing, I panicked. So I said I was calibrating the door jamb. I had heard those words before, and I was impressed with the sound of "calibrating." My goal was to get all his tools, and if you used the word "calibrating" it sounded like you needed a lot of tools.

I offered to go get him another beer while he got his tools. Moments later I was in my living room, spreading out my score and trying to figure out what I had. I recognized the basics. Hammer, saw, and the thingamajig that I had seen before. It was now time to apply the tools of the trade.

My first project was to make myself a closet organizer. I didn't have a lot of stuff to organize, but everyone said I should have a closet organizer. I knew there was a bunch of wood hidden in the grass in the backyard because I had banged my foot on it earlier. I was getting calluses on my toes just from walking in the yard.

Before I could start my closet organizer, I had to detach the Morning Glory from the boards. I got to use a hacksaw for the first time to cut those babies loose. Later, I used a hammer to kill all the giant spiders that were living in my new closet organizer. By the time I got those boards out of there it was time for a break.

A couple of weeks later I finished my organizer. It leaned a bit and it didn't look like the picture in the Eaton's catalogue, but it had other custom features. Two screws that were meant to hit boards were sticking out, so I used them to hang my car keys. Another board that didn't quite get connected at the base could move, giving me more flexibility with my organizing. One board was sticking out more than the others, and that became my tie rack. All in all, it was workable and only cost me two beers to make.

Having my neighbor's tools was very motivating, so I decided to build a shed outside to store wood for my fireplace. I didn't have any firewood to store, but I figured something would come along. Once again, I got to wrestle some boards out of the tall grass and do battle with the giant spiders. This time I used my neighbor's work gloves to cut down on the spider bites and rusty nails going into my hand.

I didn't have a plan for how the shed should look, because the remaining boards were going to pretty much dictate the outcome. When it was finished, I hesitated to come to any sort of conclusion regarding the success of the project. Naturally, friends and neighbors didn't hesitate to give their two cents worth. The most commonly asked question was, "What is it?" and the most common solution was, "Why don't you tear it down and build a shed to store firewood?"

The experience was humbling. I thought maybe if I put a few logs in it, this might help the shed through its identity crisis. That idea only led to more comments like, "Looks like the ceiling caved in," and, "I bet if you rip that thing down you could sell this place for more money." In the end I did what any handyman would have done if they were in my place: I blamed it on my neighbor's tools.

Chapter 15

The City Strikes Back

I had received my third and final notice from the City to cut my lawn. I knew it had to be cut, but how do you cut grass that's three feet tall? I'd have to rent a threshing machine from Saskatchewan to do the job.

The City work crew showed up in two vehicles. They had three lawn mowers and a bunch of Weed Whackers going at it. The six of them spent all day working on my lawn. They had to replace the blades on the mowers several times because they kept hitting all my hidden toe-stubbers. They sure were a sweaty bunch who cursed a lot.

I swear I saw some Morning Glory pull a Weed Whacker that was leaning against a fence into its lair. I guess that's Mother Nature's way of fighting back.

The fence fell down and trapped one guy because there wasn't any more Morning Glory left to support it. We got him out OK, but he sure had a lot of splinters on one side of his body. All the commotion caused a whole bunch of grouse to come running out of the long grass. They circled around and then ran back into a thick patch of grass on the other side. I wondered if I was supposed to declare this place a bird sanctuary or something?

Anyway, I was in a resting mode so I sat back and watched the activities unfold around me. I was just finishing the last of my six-pack when the work crew converged on me in my $5 chair. They presented me with a City invoice. It was for the standard lawn cutting fee set down by legislation: $25. I asked them if they would please come back again next week. A few days later I got another letter from City Hall asking for their $25 payment for cutting my lawn. I felt like they earned it and I had every intention of paying, except I didn't have any money. So I wrote back to at least acknowledge their services.

One of the other items their lawn mower blades had found was a boy's bicycle. The blade had slashed the tire and bent the rim. I really didn't care because I didn't want the bike anyway. One of my neighbors offered to buy the bike from me for $25. Sure, I said. He said it would cost about $50 to fix the tire and the rim. I mentioned this in my letter to the City.

A week later I received a cheque in the mail for $25 from City Hall as the "balance owing on my account."

Chapter 16

BBQ Season

As I watched the City crew cut my lawn, I had noticed them piling up a lot of rocks over in one corner. Afterwards, I went over to inspect the large pile. They were all brown on one side where they must have been sitting in the ground, and all of them had a new shiny top on the other side where the City workers had used them to slow down their lawn mower blades.

All of a sudden I had this craving for steak and corn, and that's when I knew I was looking at my future BBQ. I'd make a round BBQ of stone. Dirty side facing in and shiny side facing out. But this time I was going to do it the handyman way. I was going to use concrete. I had never used concrete before, but I figured how hard could it be? I went to the hardware store and grabbed a bucket and trowel in one hand, and then reached down to pick up a bag of cement with the other. It never budged. I thought it was stuck to the other bags until I realized it weighed more than me. It was the smallest bag they had. I wondered if my neighbor had any cement.

Sure enough, one of my neighbors did, complete with bucket and shovel. I never even gave them a beer. They were so happy I had cut the lawn that they said I could borrow from them anytime. I noticed they had a wheelbarrow. I didn't need one, but I asked if I could borrow it anyway.

I really didn't have much trouble making the BBQ. It was only a foot tall. I even had a BBQ grill. One of the City workers had found it with his lawn mower blade. I just used my neighbor's hammer to bang the grill back into shape. The frame of my old bed had been stacked in a corner by the City crew. I broke off some of that wood to make a fire to grill my dinner.

While I was having my steak and corn that night, I was thinking about maybe building a shed to house all my new tools.

Chapter 17

Rules of the House

If you've ever bought and moved into a house all by yourself, you'll know where I'm coming from. (If you haven't, just fantasize for the rest of this chapter.) You soon learn that all the "Rules of the House" are good ones because you get to make them yourself. I mean, why would you want to make a bad rule? This is an important phenomenon because it explains a lot of things.

For instance, it's okay to store dirty dishes in the oven if company is coming over and you have no time to wash them. Most people think you have to wash them so the place looks clean, but you can see from my method that, not only do you get the same results, you save a lot of valuable time.

Hosting small dinner parties for friends brought on another Rule of the House: "Please offer to bring something and I will take you up on your offer and tell you what it is." When properly orchestrated, a good time can be had by all, with no expenses incurred by the host. In reality, people just want someone to coordinate a good time. That's what I do. A helpful hint is to invite someone who also owns a fireplace. Let them know you're out of wood and get them to bring a couple of logs over. Also, leftovers from the meal are very important. As a bachelor, you must perfect the droopy-eye "I-have-no-food-if-you-take-that-home" look. It's a dinner bonus and a survival must.

If there are no dinner plans in sight, then groceries take on a set of rules. Like buying food that already comes in a container. You save valuable time by not having to put it in a pot to heat and back on a dish to eat. No dishes are a bonus. Same theory as pizza.

Depending on whether you have a plumbing or electrical problem in the house, it always makes sense to invite these kinds of people over. You know, the ones that can fix anything. The rules sway in favor of the guest in these instances. A typical invite is, "Hey, Joe, I got some beers in the fridge and the game's on tonight. Come on over." The great thing about sports is there's always an intermission or a halftime with not much to do. See where I'm going with this?

There is an established universal law that states, "The more people who know what it is you want, the better the chance you have of getting it." I think this is where the term "networking" came into existence. Same thing, just a shorter word. Anyway, this is why people buy things for you at garage sales and give you things out of their basements they don't use anymore. It's true that none of my plates or glasses match, but that doesn't make them functionally deficient. I think the term "new wave" best describes my table setting. Ironically, you're giving out a strong message to everyone on your needs, come Christmas and birthdays. It prevents getting socks and underwear from Mom.

The Right to Relax rule is always in effect. There would be less stress in people's lives if everyone paid more attention to this rule. Yes, you can wear your shoes in the house and yes, you can put them up on the coffee table. My furniture does not have much value, and you couldn't possibly scratch or stain it any worse than it already is, so just relax. Yes, you can chew with your mouth open and yes, you can scratch wherever it itches.

If I wanted everyone to be as proper as the Queen of England, I wouldn't have any friends, so just relax, will you?

Chapter 18

Sprinkler System

I didn't own a hose or anything else that would water a lawn. So even though I had never put in an underground sprinkler system, I decided to go for it. Mainly because my brother Dan worked at a plumbing supply place, and he got me a bunch of stuff that was basically going to be thrown out because it was outdated and didn't fit in with their new sales line. That made the cost to me right up my alley.

It was definitely a hodgepodge of stuff, but since I didn't know what a quality system looked like, I figured it wouldn't make much difference. It was going to be buried under the ground anyway, so who cared what it looked like? Naturally, it didn't come with any instructions, because the stuff came from the bottom of several bins. I prefer to do things without instructions anyway. I like the challenge, and having to read instructions just slows you down.

I laid the pipe around the yard so I could catch every corner with water. It was a very complicated maze when I was done. There were going to be twelve heads that would pop right out of the ground and start spraying, if my planning was right. My brother Dan told me to dig at least twelve inches deep so that the pipes wouldn't freeze in the winter.

So that's what I did. The sun was starting to go down and I hadn't finished the first line, which was one of the shorter ones. This was supposed to be a weekend project, with me having the afternoons off. This was not going according to plan. The rest of the water lines were only about three inches deep. I figured that if one froze, I'd still have eleven left. The project was going much quicker now.

When I finally got the last of them in and hooked up, I couldn't wait to turn it on to bask in the glory of my accomplishment. Unfortunately, the water line from the house didn't work. I never thought to test it out before starting the project. My brother Dan came to the rescue. He said the good news is that you have an outside tap. The bad news is that there's no plumbing whatsoever behind it. It would have to be totally redone. I asked him if he wanted a beer, and how long would it take him to fix it?

Well, we finally got it all hooked up. Here was this pipe, the newest feature of my house, and you couldn't see it because it was hidden in the basement. The time came to test my sprinkler system. This time the knob that was meant to turn didn't, and snapped off instead. That set us back another two hours. I figured nothing could stand in my way now. We turned it on and nothing happened.

My brother walked around the yard trying to figure out what was wrong. That's when I told him there were twelve of the little babies scattered all over the yard. He asked me if I had ever heard of water pressure. He sat me down and explained it. I was not a happy camper.

I went out and bought a hose and a sprinkler. It worked just fine.

Chapter 19

Revenue Canada

I had never really thought much about income tax. Just gave my T4 to anyone who would fill out the form for me. It was plus or minus $100 every time. Now things were different. I had receipts and bank statements and things I had never had to use before. And now I was in a deal-direct situation with Revenue Canada. They asked me where my records were.

"They're beside my stereo," I said.

"Go get them."

"What do you want to hear?"

The interest on my mortgage was tax-deductible. The hose and sprinkler were tax-deductible. Beer and pizza weren't tax-deductible. They asked me so many questions I thought sooner or later they're going to want a blood sample. I had only scheduled eight minutes for this, and I was already into my second hour of interrogation.

When it was all over, they said I was getting an $1,800 refund. I asked them to check the numbers again or get me someone who knew how to fill the form out correctly. They said there was no mistake. I told them I didn't have a first child to give them. They insisted I send in the form and accept the money graciously. On that day, I fell in love with Revenue Canada. But I didn't want to buy stock in this company because they gave their money away too easily.

Revenue Canada was aces in my books. I was looking forward to many more years dealing with them.

Chapter 20

Project Planning Time

There are turning points in your life when it's "in with the bad" and "out with the bad." I mean something new enters your life that scares the socks off you but, when you look around, something that used to scare you doesn't anymore. I think they call it maturing or growing up. (Or being really naive, or getting older...whatever.)

It's kind of like the lightbulb in my head that went on every so often. It was a scary thought because it didn't mean I had a *good* idea. It only meant I had an idea. There was a twofold test that every idea had to pass. The first question was: "Will my bank cover this?" and the second question was: "Do I need a special kind of insurance for this?" About half my ideas failed this test, but the ones that did make it to the second stage were what I would call suspicious. For example, ideas involving electricity, plumbing or wood.

Anyway, this idea somehow passed the test: it was time to start a project. I had felt it coming on for a long time now, so I knew I had to answer the call. I decided to replace my sundeck with a bigger one. The old one was not only too small, it was so old it had a warning sticker on it like the cigarette packages have. I was too scared to tell my insurance company about it.

I took a long, hard look at the deck. Suddenly, different parts of my body started to act up. My fingers started throbbing and I believe they were trying to send the message, *"Remember the hammer, don't start a project."* My thighs with the screwdriver holes in them were sending messages as well. My brain was trying to scatter my thought patterns, and was telling me to go into the fridge and have a beer and relax. I suddenly realized how many body parts had been intimately associated with so many projects. They were all pleading for me to change my mind, but I would have no part of it.

First, I needed a plan. I knew I needed one because all the How To books said I did. So I put pen to paper and worked it out. I was surprised at how easy it was. I only had to put down two words: "Doug" was one; and "Dad" was the other. Doug, my brother-in-law, was a carpenter who would help me because my sister Terri would make him. And Dad would help me with the finances as well as the construction because I was his son, and that's what dads do. The plan was complete and, as far as I was concerned, flawless. So I went for the beer my brain had told me was in the fridge.

Chapter 21

Project Implementation Time

It was only a week later that I had my two unsuspecting project helpers with their wives (my Mom and sister) over for dinner. The weather was hot and the beer was ice-cold. Somehow, we were outside underneath the deck, and I was commenting on the structure. Both Doug and Dad commented on how I should just rip the old thing down and start all over. So I asked them, "With both of you being carpenters, in your professional opinion, what kind of deck would you build?" Luckily, I had two pencils and some paper so that they could start to sketch the new deck right away.

By about 11:00 that night we had a complete list of all the items I would ever need. Every piece of wood and every pound of nails was accounted for. It seemed like an awful lot of stuff, and I wondered just how I was going to get all this material. I just couldn't see myself doing it. So I moved to the next stage of my plan. I took five copies of the list and attached a short letter to each. The letters were addressed to Home Hardware-type places that would have all this stuff, and basically said, "How much would it cost me to have all this stuff purchased and delivered?" I emphasized "quality products" to be on the safe side. I figured, how would I know if I got good wood unless I made it sound like I knew what I was talking about?

Two weeks went by and I had all five quotes back. Surprisingly, they would all do it, and they all gave me a price. I didn't want to spend too much time on this, so I phoned the lowest bidder and said if he could knock off another $100, I would take his quote. He did, and two days later I had all the stuff. Part of the deal was for them to set up an account with me and I would make payment upon completion of the project. Somehow, they thought I was some kind of contractor who did this for a living, so they were real happy to set me up with an account. Next thing I knew, I got another five percent discount because I was some sort of preferred client and they wanted me as a long-term customer. I figured this was a bad time to ask for How To books on building decks. Whatever; I took the five percent. So far, the deck hadn't cost a cent.

The next phase was to demolish the old deck. I figured this was the perfect job for me. There seemed to be something natural that I felt about this part of the project. The question still remained: what was the fastest and easiest method of demolishing the deck? I started to realize I was always looking for the fastest and easiest way to do things. There was probably a direct ratio between the number of accidents I'd had and how fast the job got done. Probably the same ratio for the quality of my output. Didn't matter; I still wanted a fast and easy way of doing this, so I tied a rope to the bumper of my car and fastened it to the deck. I figured I could do the job while sitting down.

Well, I drove down the road and heard the big bang I was anticipating. It had more of a metal crashing sound than a wood crashing sound, though. Sure enough, the old deck was still standing, and my bumper was in the middle of the road with the rope still attached to it. On my next attempt, I tied the rope to something under the car. I don't know the name of the part I attached it to, but I knew I would need another one just like it when I saw it lying in the road, too. I figured I should try something else before I had no car left. Experience-wise, if I ever had to demolish a car, I'd know exactly how to do it.

I ended up using crowbars and a series of battering rams to demolish the deck. If I'd just had a small nuclear device, I could have gotten it done in no time. I sure had enough wood for my woodshed now! A whole deck's worth–and we're talking seasoned wood here.

I should have listened to my body parts.

Chapter 22

Project Construction

We actually had a lot of fun putting up the deck. Doug and Dad knew exactly what to do. As the project leader, I stayed out of their way and made sure there were lots of pizzas and cold beers. When it came to cutting boards, we realized after my first attempt that this would not be my permanent job. After a few other attempts at tasks involving deck-building, we all realized that I would be the "Nailer of Things." I was proud of this title, and I proceeded to make a loop in my belt to hold the hammer. Nails would go in the back pocket. All things would be nailed by me.

We were proceeding along as planned when I noticed a man standing in the yard admiring our work. I asked him what he thought of the deck and if he lived around here. He said the deck looked great and that he was from City Hall. Up until now, most of my dealings with City Hall had been good. But that was to change: I was about to enter the world of Building Permits.

Now, I'm a reasonable kind of guy. But that doesn't help when dealing with City Hall. I'm also very patient. Unfortunately, I lost that in a real hurry. I don't even want to go into the details. Suffice it to say that the project took a one-month holiday. It was smack dab in the middle of my BBQ season, so I was not a happy camper. When we finally finished the deck, it ended up looking just the same as it would have whether it had a building permit or not. I framed the building permit and hung it on the deck. Oh yeah, a safety tip for any of you would-be Nailers of Things. Nails in the back pocket aren't a good idea.

There was still time to do one more stupid thing before I called it a day. I went over to my local hardware store where they had planter boxes on sale. I bought a really long one made out of wood to attach to my new balcony. I didn't have any brackets to support it, so I just put a bunch of screws into the planter box and attached it to the outside of the balcony. Next, I filled it full of dirt and planted all my new flowers that were on sale, and gave it a good watering. Looked real good.

The next day when I went out to survey my new deck, all the plants were gone. I walked over to the planter box and looked into a big nothing, including no bottom. By looking through the hole in my planter box I could see the flowers, dirt, and the bottom of my planter box splattered all over the ground below. The bottom just couldn't handle the weight.

I don't usually drink a beer before nine in the morning.

Chapter 23

Loose Ends

In amongst all the rest of the tools I had collected from my neighbor, I noticed that he also owned a Robertson screwdriver. I figured there was no reason to have two of the same tool in my house and, since I still had the bill, I took mine back for a refund.

I received a letter from City Hall about my Property Taxes being in arrears. Believe it or not, when they first told me how much I owed, I thought they were kidding. I thought maybe I should send them a bill for bending my BBQ grill with their lawn mower. Heck, I could blame the broken planter box on their Building Permit while I was at it. "Structurally unsound and pending lawsuit" might get their attention. Flowers gave their life – fighting for their Building Permit rights!

The retired couple who lived next to me (the ones who had lent me their wheelbarrow) were really nice. Their lawn was like a putting green. If they found a weed in their lawn they almost had an argument about who got to pull it. They also had a big garden with lots of corn on the cob. One day they offered me a whole basketful. I said thanks and asked if I could borrow their shovel.

That night I had my friends over for a BBQ. I asked them to supply the steaks and I would supply the corn. Steaks barbecued over cherry wood make for an awesome flavor. (I had already used the last of my bed to BBQ.)

Chapter 24

The Years Go By

It had been a couple of years and I was getting along with my downstairs tenants just fine. They were only four months' rent in arrears, down from six. The lawn was back to an acceptable length, and I was the proud owner of a lawn mower. It was one of those electric ones because I didn't want to hurt myself with a gas one. There were no electrical outlets outside the house, so we just ran a cord out my kitchen window. The mower wasn't working at the moment, because we ran over the cord and cut it in two.

I had been using chemicals on my Morning Glory for two years now. It was working, but you have to realize that the root system it establishes is as thick as a telephone pole. I needed a cubic yard of dirt to fill in the holes it left when I tried to remove it. I hate the name "Morning Glory."

One day the City put a sidewalk in on our street. I was impressed with the improvement this made to my place. The increase to my Property Taxes will take care of the costs, they told me.

I got to renew the term of my mortgage. Interest rates had been down since I signed up at fourteen percent for two years, but now they were back up again. For some reason, there was a Mideast scare about oil prices and, since the banks were worried what this was going to do to the economy, they decided to raise interest rates. I used electric heat. I was lucky if I bought one quart of oil a year. I had never been to the Mideast, but it was going to cost me $4,000 more in interest.

I bought a greenhouse for the backyard. Planted tomatoes and green vegetables. Forgot about them for a few days and they got toasted by the sun. Turned the greenhouse into a storage shed.

I tried to repair the leak in my roof. I got the thickest, gooiest stuff they had to fill in anything that looked like a crack or a hole. The roof was flat and covered with tar and gravel. I saw a couple of low points and decided to fill them in. When I stepped back to admire my work, I tripped over the tar bucket. If I had still been wearing my Robertson screwdriver in my belt, it would have sheared my leg off. Fortunately, landing on a tar and gravel roof on a hot, sunny day makes for a soft landing. I now had a new low spot on the roof, and I had already used up the last of the tar.

A few weeks later it rained. I still had Old Faithful dripping behind my bedroom wall, but now there was a new sound. It was more of a flowing sound, as opposed to that irritating dripping sound. When I thumbed through the yellow pages looking for roof repair people, the pages were sticking to the tar I still couldn't get off my hand.

I bought one of those potted trees for Christmas. I thought, hey, I can have a Christmas tree and then plant it on the property to increase the value. The dog downstairs thought it was a good idea too. The poor tree never made it to springtime.

I read about a seminar on "Making Money Through Real Estate Investments." It was free. I thought anything that's free can't be all that bad.

Chapter 25

Strange Feeling

I received all my mortgage documents from my bank in the mail. One of the documents hit me right on the side of the head (figuratively speaking). It was a strange feeling. Not the kind where my brain hurts when I try to fend off reality, but this sensation left me in a stunned state. It was a good stunned feeling.

You see, my net worth a couple of years before had been $255. Remember, I found the chair for $5? Well, except for adding a used lawn mower to my assets, I still figured I was worth under $300. But here was this document from the bank telling me I was now appraised at $97,500! Hey, I only paid $80,900. You mean you're telling me I made $16,600, and all I did was cut the lawn and wreck the roof?

It was *Twilight Zone* day because sitting right there on my wooden hydro cable coffee table was that old newspaper article about "Making Money Through Real Estate Investments." The seminar was that night. I looked for the newspaper to see what my horoscope read. I forgot I only got the paper on Sundays, because that was when the funnies came out.

I knew I had a date with Destiny that night. I'd have to cancel with her so I could go to the seminar.

Chapter 26

The Twilight Zone

I kept humming space lunar sounds from *The Twilight Zone* as I made my way to the ballroom at the hotel. There were hundreds of us, drones all drawn and programmed to enter and listen to our new leader. Somebody elbowed me and told me to shut up and stop making those noises.

The speaker was excellent. He made promises, but didn't tell you exactly how it worked. He showed examples of people making millions of dollars and hardly lifting a finger. I missed a lot of the seminar because I started daydreaming about owning all the houses on my block. I'd sure get a lot more respect if I owned all the houses this guy said I should.

He really got my attention with some simple math. It was the kind of math I understood. I understood it because it had just happened to me. I put $8,000 down on a house and made $16,600. So if I took that equity out of my house, I could buy two more houses. Two years later, assuming the same pattern occurred, I would buy six more houses to bring my total to nine. And so on and so on, until I owned my whole street in six or so years. He talked about a ten-year plan, but I figured I could do it in six.

Of course, there was one problem. He wanted $500 for his weekend seminar. If I could sell my chair, I'd only have to come up with $495, I thought. It was no use. But when I got home, *The Twilight Zone* smacked me on the side of the head again. There was my tenant with $500 CASH for his rent. I had never seen him with cash before. I knew what I had to do. Things would be just too weird if I didn't. I got myself back to the hotel. No one was in the room. I remember thinking to myself that it was just as well, $500 was an awful lot to pay for one weekend of learning. As I glanced over to the lobby, there he was.

I signed up.

Chapter 27

Teach Me, O Great One

I was nervous and maybe a little scared. I figured those were natural feelings prior to becoming a millionaire land baron.

The seminar was held in a university auditorium. There were about a hundred of us. This guy stepped up to the podium and introduced himself as our speaker for the next two days. "What happened to the other guy?" I thought. The one I gave the $500 to. The one who was to personally teach me all the secrets of real estate investment. Where's my guru? Who's this cheap copy?

Well, after I got over that, I found out this guy was pretty good. The course was intense and didn't make my brain hurt. I now had so much knowledge I didn't know where to start. I mean, I now knew all about distressed property sales, cash flow, overdrafts, equity lending and assumable loans. I homed in on my telephone tactics, negotiation skills and buying strategies. I was ready to squeeze a foreclosure, bargain at an auction block, liquidate, and go into syndication. I was poised for a hostile takeover.

So I immediately used one of his theories and called my brother Dan. He had lots of money. I couldn't wait to tell Dan about all the bikini-clad babes who hang around guys with lots of Real Estate...**guys like us!**

Chapter 28

My Bro

"Dan, my man. How's my bro?"

"What do you want?" he asked.

Dan is my younger brother by about twelve years. What on Earth were my parents thinking about when they decided to have him? But he turned out to be a good kid. Other than meeting for family dinners, Dan and I never did anything together. Too much of an age thing. Even when Dan had a good-paying job, he was always at someone else's house for a free hot meal. I called him cheap, but Mom called him thrifty. Bottom line is I knew he must have some money stashed away, which made him the perfect business partner.

"Got a business proposal for you."

"How much is it going to cost me?"

Well, we got together to discuss real estate. I caught him at a good time because he didn't have anything to invest his money in. He wouldn't say how much he had, but it didn't matter, because I would take whatever he had. Now, I wasn't trying to pull a fast one on my brother. No way Mom would let me get away with that. I would save the fast ones for other people.

Before he knew what had happened, Dan and I were looking at real estate. It was great because I could afford a lot more with his money. The idea was for us to use his money to buy some revenue property. The plan was to get a multi-unit building, and we would split the rent we received. When it came to the mortgage payments, I would be paying something like ninety percent of it because Dan had come up with the deposit. So the bottom line was that we both owned half of it; it's just that Dan owned more of his half than I did of mine. A lot more.

The banks liked it because both of us would be responsible (or another way of looking at it was that the banks would be able to catch at least one of us if the other skipped town). Dan liked it because he wasn't alone with his very first purchase. Don't forget, Dan was just turning twenty-two when I scooped him.

We knew we were destined to be business partners. We were warned about doing business with family, but when Dan found out how much I knew about things like Morning Glory, fixing roofs, and screwdrivers, he knew he'd picked the right guy.

Besides, I'm his bro!

Chapter 29

The Hunt Is On... Again

Dan and I spent the evening mapping out our strategy. We knew the areas of town we wanted to look in, and we sort of knew our price range. We had a "shop 'til you drop" attitude. We would pound the pavement until we got the deal of the century. We would have nothing less than a dozen real estate agents working for us. We were focused, we were pumped.

Dad dropped by that night and showed us a brochure for a house that was for sale in the paper. The next day Dan and I bought it. The paperwork was completed by lunchtime, so Dan and I played some tennis.

Now, this place was big. It was a side-by-side duplex, three stories high on both sides. The top two levels were rented out, and the bottom level on each side was unfinished. It was a perfect opportunity to put in a couple of illegal suites. I didn't like to use the term "illegal" in front of Dan. I mean, this was only his second day in business with his brother and we were already doing something illegal.

We got several estimates to see how much it would cost to do all this illegal stuff, and I could see that my brother was starting to wonder what we had gotten ourselves into. But when I showed him how much money we could make by having four suites instead of two, he decided to go along with it. I decided to stop using the word "illegal," and started using "nonconforming" instead.

We paid $140,000 for this monster place. It was only ten years old, as opposed to my place, which had been built just a couple of months after Columbus discovered America. The scary thing about this whole thing was that this place was only two blocks away from my house. And, I'm not kidding you, it was on the same street. Yup, my dream of owning the whole block was starting to shape up.

When we went to finance this place, we went to a different bank than the one I was dealing with. Dan was confused because he thought we should deal with my bank, as they knew me there. I didn't tell him, but that was the exact reason we weren't dealing with my bank. They knew me there.

This time around, I had a lot of fun. Dan had $40,000 cash to put down on the place, which was more than we needed. You could tell the bank manager was happy with the down payment. When he asked me how much I was putting down on the place I said, "Nothing." We all broke out in laughter and then, after drying his eyes, he said, "Seriously, how much are you putting down?"

Later, I got the impression that they were inventing forms for us to fill out just because they didn't like me. They always asked Dan if he wanted a cup of coffee, then they would turn to me and give me another form to fill out. They even called me at home and said I had to come in to initial a change. Dan never had to come in.

Well, we had to see a lawyer to finalize everything. Dan said, "Let's use the same lawyer you used last time." I said that wasn't a good idea. Same reason as the bank. Dan and I had a lot of planning to do, so we bought a six-pack, ordered pizza, and got down to business.

Chapter 30

Strategy Time

I learned from my brother-in-law Ben that you've got to know the right people. If you don't, it will cost you an arm and a leg to get things done. So, keeping that in mind, Dan and I asked for lots of estimates to get those suites built and rented out. Plus, it's a great way of getting ideas from contractors, but it was going to cost way too much, so we went to Plan B. We would do it ourselves.

Plan B scared everyone in the family and all of our close friends. Dan and I weren't scared because we saw how much it would cost for Plan A. Our strategy was to get people to help us. We were going with Ben's theory. Now this wasn't going to be easy, because who wants to help build a suite from scratch at our going wage, which was nothing?

So, what we did was invite people over to our new place to celebrate the new investment with free beer and pizza. The first person on our list was my brother-in-law Doug. Not only did he know carpentry, but he once wired a whole house. We needed an electrician, and Doug liked beer and pizza. Dad used to be a carpenter. He also liked beer and pizza. Fortunately, Dan, my business partner and brother, knew plumbing. Didn't matter if he liked beer and pizza because he didn't have much choice in the matter. Ben had to help because it was his theory, and my other brother Ken was a beer and pizza fan, too. As for me, I rounded out the field as the handyman. I liked beer and pizza.

Before you knew it, everyone was wearing a tool belt with a hammer in it, a slice of pizza in one hand and a beer in the other. This went on for nearly four months.

Chapter 31

Caution, Construction Zone

Thank goodness we did this project during the winter. There's never much to do anyway during that time, so we might as well be working on a project.

Everyone worked their day jobs and would then start to show up at the house. We hooked up a fridge and that baby never had less than two hundred cans of beer in it at a time. Every night there was a delivery man bringing something for dinner. Music blared in the background, and those power tools were happening. Every corner had a heater, so we stayed toasty during the cold weather.

Some nights we lost track of time and worked until three in the morning. Our new tenants upstairs knew we were the Landlords, so they didn't say much. Heck, they even paid the electric bills so we could run all our stuff.

Dan and I started a ledger to keep track of all the costs. The dollar amount in the Beer, Pizza and Miscellaneous Foods columns kept right up there with the Building Materials column. Heck, we had some take-out food restaurants that wanted to open an account with us. We even figured out that it would have been cheaper to buy a brewery instead of paying the going rate at the liquor stores. Nevertheless, with us paying the ultimate minimum wage rate of nothing, we had to keep the work crew happy, and that's just what we did.

People were always dropping by to say hello, have a beer, and scrimmage through the various food groups that were accumulating in the fridge. They knew we had the best-stocked fridge in town, and we didn't do salads. Dan and I always played the host, but before the visitors even knew what was happening, they found themselves with a hammer in one hand and a work belt wrapped around their waist with twenty pounds of nails in it. We used the standard line, "When the nails are all used up, you can go." We even had a pizza delivery guy on his last run at 1:00 in the morning helping us out. He was looking at us putting in a door frame and was bold enough to say, "Oh, I've done that before."

I handed him a beer and said, "Prove it." Not only did he prove it, but he came back the next day on his day off to finish the job!

It was funny. People didn't mind doing this. Everyone seemed to be learning something and having a good time doing it. And everyone always had a full belly attached to a semi-conscious mind. Dan and I always knew when the cut-off point was for power tools and electrical stuff. There was always a job waiting for someone with a fuzzy IQ from the beer, and we would steer them in that direction. Lucky for me, I only lived two blocks away. I had a fifty-fifty chance of walking home safely.

Chapter 32

My Learning Curve

I learned a lot during those four months in the Construction Zone. Some of the more memorable lessons were:
- Wire cutters can travel at the speed of light when they make contact with live wires (we still don't know where that pair went). I don't do electricity. You have to realize that I came to that conclusion very easily. I can't see the darn thing coming, smell it, or taste it. You can only feel it, and that is far, far too late to do you any good.
- When using a hammer, if you hit the same finger in exactly the same spot you did before, the pain actually doubles.
- Contact glue, when properly applied between your fingers, will keep them together for days.
- Always screw in the drain plug of a water heater before you turn the water on.
- Buying steel-toed work boots after all your toes are smashed up is too late.
- Measure four times, cut once. Repeat if necessary.
- Hold light fixtures firmly with one hand when installing, or they can and will drop on your head.
- Five male workers become instantly useless if a girl wearing a tank top puts on a tool belt to help out.
- Do not install insulation yourself. Don't even think about it. Get someone else to do it.
- Put as many screwdrivers as you want in your tool belt...you'll still be missing the one you need.
- Always put an elastic band around your can of beer to help

identify it from everyone else's.
- In between bites, always place your pizza slice on top of your beer can to keep the dust from going into your beer (topping side should face up).
- You can increase the beer-holding capacity of your fridge if you remove the built-in egg holder on the inside door.
- A powerful drill will go through wood faster and wrench your wrist easier when it hits a knot. It will always hit a knot.
- Always keep a fake head of lettuce in the fridge in case Mom drops by to see how you're eating.
- Electrical wires being fed through holes will wrap around and poke you in the eye when you least expect it.
- Everything, and I mean everything, can be delivered to your door if you really want it to.
- All tools secretly move around at night and hide.

These lessons would end up being the building blocks and foundation that would give me the mistaken confidence to propel myself into a whole new series of future projects I really had no business starting.

Chapter 33

Things Happen!

The day finally came. We were finished. Our beer and pizza days were behind us. It was a true team effort. We had built two identical suites, each containing a kitchen, bathroom, bedroom and living room. They were great-looking suites, and Dan and I swore that we would only rent them out to people who had the proper attitude about keeping them clean and in good shape.

As you can tell, we were incredibly out of touch with reality. We didn't know then that "things happen." "Things happen" was a very broad category that best describes the depreciation of our suites over the next ten years. Here are some classic examples:

Landlord: "How come there's a hole in the bathroom door?"

Tenant: "How did that get there? Honey, have you noticed this hole before?"

Landlord: "You said you would cut the lawn."

Tenant: "The lawn mower's broken. Someone ran over the cord."

Landlord: "It worked perfectly fine when I put it away last week."

Tenant: "I think I should get paid more for cutting the lawn."

Landlord: "You haven't cut the lawn. You've only managed to cut the cord so far."

Tenant: "I used part of the rent money to replace the mirror in the hallway."

Landlord: "Why did you replace the mirror in the hallway?"

Tenant: "It was broken."

Landlord: "How did it break?"

Tenant: "I guess it was just old."

When "things happen," there is always time and money involved.

The time was always right now, and the cost to fix the "things that happen" seemed to be totally irrelevant to the people who make "things happen." Within two years the suites needed new paint. The new appliances looked sad without their knobs and switches. Every corner of the bathroom looked like it had a science project growing in it.

For the next few years Dan and I were what you would call living on the edge. Mainly because "things happen." Like this one day when I noticed seven holes in our wooden sundeck railing. I asked the tenant how they got there.

"Beats me," he says, "they've always been there."

Later, when I was leaving, I noticed a very nice (and brand new) wooden board screwed to a wall in the entranceway. It had exactly seven hooks screwed into it for hanging coats. I said, "What a coincidence, that's exactly how many holes are in my sundeck railing. I'll bet they're spaced apart exactly the same as your coat hooks." Well, the color on his face pretty well told the story. He had drilled the holes for his coat rack on my railing and the drill bit did its thing.

When things happen, they happen in color too. Like this big red paint stain on our driveway I couldn't help but notice. "This thing's going to attract UFOs," I told them. "It's the brightest, reddest red I've ever seen, and it's not going to fade away in my lifetime." I could see them fiddling with their best "I didn't do it" excuse until they saw me looking at their kid's wagon, which happened to be the exact same color.

Okay, so now I'm calm and I accept the fact that things happen. "Putty in these holes, put another coat of stain on the board, and paint the driveway while you're at it, and let's call it a day."

Chapter 34

Tenants

The world according to tenants is a strange one. It was like we were in different time zones and spoke a different language. For instance, the majority of phone calls from them were between 6:30 and 7:30 p.m. when I was having dinner. I don't recall ever finishing my dinner without it being stone cold. The rest of the phone calls were between 11:00 at night and 6:00 in the morning. Nothing broke or needed replacing during regular daylight hours.

When I was working on the place, the tenants would always hang around me, giving me their input on how they would do the job. They never volunteered to help, but they were quick to point out my faults. The opposite was true when it was time to collect the rent. There wouldn't be a soul in sight for days.

I'd like to say that collecting rent was always a hit or miss situation. The fact of the matter is that it was always a miss. From the five sets of tenants I had, I almost never got all the rent at the beginning of the month. On the few occasions that I actually did, half the cheques bounced anyway.

Finally, one day I got to the end of my rope and decided to give one particular set of tenants an eviction notice. Well, they thought they had the right to be three months in arrears on paying rent, and the next thing I knew, I got a call from the Tenancy Branch saying that this situation was going to arbitration. Tenants have their own branch. I asked where the Landlords' Branch was located, but I didn't get an answer.

I thought, "What a waste of time." But if I needed an arbitrator to force my tenants to pay rent, so be it.

Chapter 35

Arbitration: Tenants 1, Landlord 0

I couldn't believe that the arbitrator ruled in favor of the tenants. This arbitrator felt sorry for their financial woes, and asked me to work out a schedule for them to make payments. I told her I already had a schedule. It involved paying rent once a month at the beginning of each month.

She saw the tenant agreement that spelled it all out. It was signed and agreed to by all parties. Apparently that didn't matter. To add insult to injury, she wanted me to reimburse the tenant for the $35 fee for filing the arbitration because she had ruled in their favor. Two weeks later, at the end of the month, the tenants left without a trace. They left behind a mess and I never saw them again.

Now help me with this, everyone. What part of the "tenant agreement" didn't the arbitrator understand? I mean, does this agreement protect us both by setting out basic principles like, "I'll borrow a couple of hundred thousand dollars and buy a house so that you can consider paying some rent while you're living there."? Or, "I'll hold a couple hundred dollars for a damage deposit, but if the damage costs exceed that, don't worry, I'll take care of it."? I mean, this overall concept is bad enough without this kind of thing happening.

Well, unfortunately, there was only one thing to learn from this. And that was to cut your losses, meaning that on day one, if you don't get your rent, they get an eviction notice. Not the way I wanted to do business, but that's the message I got from the arbitrator.

I know that's how I felt at that moment, but that's not how I really am. I have as much compassion for people's circumstances as the next guy. Dad was right there for me when I told him how I felt. I'll never forget what he said: "That's good of you, son. It's good you feel for your fellow man like that. But it's going to cost you money."

And it did.

Chapter 36

Appliances

I never really thought much about appliances until they started to break down. One day I was staring at a broken refrigerator with my tenant standing behind me. I had the door open and I was looking inside. She probably thought I was looking for the problem but, as habits go, when I stare into a fridge I'm looking for something to eat. So in this case, I was looking at her food. You can tell a lot about someone by looking at what they have in their refrigerator.

It was all standard food stuff. Three ketchup bottles with all of them having more ketchup smeared on the outside than on the inside. One large jar of pickles with one pickle in it. Chinese food take-out containers with chow mein hanging down the side, and a block of butter with jam smeared on one end. I could have easily mistaken their fridge for mine, except I always had a pizza box in mine, with beer in the crisper. The only time I had lettuce in my fridge was to cover up the beer cans in the crisper so that my friends wouldn't see them. They would never think to look under a lettuce leaf. I'm not so sure they even knew what a lettuce leaf looked like, never mind touching one.

So I'm standing there, as I often seem to do, staring at this broken appliance. I can't put my finger on the problem, but the fact of the matter is, it's broken. I don't have the time, money, patience, attitude or the skill to fix it, so I stand there looking at it. I usually start to daydream at this stage and often find myself on a tropical beach somewhere, but that usually only lasts a few minutes because the tenant says, "What should we do?" In my mind I answer, "Get a Tequila Sunrise."

With the appliance broken and me not on the beach anymore, I continue to stand there and look at the problem. "Why is this happening to me?" helps put the problem in perspective, but does nothing to solve it. "Where's my Tequila Sunrise?" doesn't help either. "What are my options?" clouds the issue and permanently removes me from the beach as I force myself to move from complete ignorance to complicated theories mixed with some kind of data input. Wrong mix for the Sunrise, too. My beers in the fridge back home are calling me. Why am I standing here?

While I was standing there I started adding it all up. There was this fridge I was staring at, and another one downstairs. Two more on the other side, and two more back at my place. That meant I owned six refrigerators. Therefore, I owned six stoves. Everyone had a hot water tank, so I had six of those. Four of the suites had washers and dryers, so that meant eight more. Four suites had dishwashers. I realized I was a flippin' used appliance salesman. No wonder I was always staring at a broken appliance. There were thirty of the stupid things, and I didn't know how to fix any of them.

I asked the tenant why she had broken my refrigerator. She said she was sorry, but I had to replace the roast that she'd had in the fridge because it went bad. "Where's the roast?" I asked. Well, they'd had it for dinner the day before and it hadn't tasted very good. "So maybe you're just not a good cook," I suggested.

Getting back to the fridge, I sure wasn't wasting any energy with the door wide open, because there certainly wasn't any cold air coming out. I decided to check the basics. Was the fridge plugged in, did the crisper close up, was the temperature gauge turned up, and did the light go out when I closed the door? Everything was as it should be. There was nothing left to do but kick the side of the fridge and hurt my foot. After that, I called in the repair people.

Repair people are sort of different. They talk to you like you're a repair person just like them. They launch right into fridge lingo and acronyms as they describe the problem. I nodded my head knowingly, waiting to hear a dollar amount (which never comes). The object of this conversation is to latch onto a couple of key words and, when you get the chance, all you have to do is rearrange the sentence using the key words. Your main purpose is to demonstrate that you understand the intricate guts of the fridge, and that you are challenging their methodology. If you're successful, you might hear the words, "Well, there is another, less expensive way to fix this." That's when you know you've hit paydirt and that the fridge will not become an economic burden.

    I thanked the repair man for fixing the fridge. He asked me if I wanted him to do anything about the dent on the side of the fridge, but I said that was okay.

    At month-end my tenant took $18 off the rent cheque for the roast.

Chapter 37

Life's Problems

My brother Dan remained my lifeline. Half of the house was his, so half the problems were his, too. There wasn't a single problem we encountered where we couldn't find a reason to break out into laughter. Whenever Dan stared at a problem he would always use his standard line: "Why me?"

We always asked the basic questions when dealing with life's little surprises. The first one was always, "Will it go away by itself?" We always hoped that the answer was yes. It was certainly the cheapest solution. If the answer was no, then the next question was, "Are we insured for this?" That was another cheap way of getting things done.

We tried to get tenants to fix things. We always reimbursed them for any costs, but in the long run, the costs far exceeded getting a professional in to fix it. For some reason, tenants figure their time is worth about $40 an hour when they work for me, but they'll work for someone else for $12.

One set of tenants asked if they could paint their living room. I said, "Sure, I'll reimburse you for the paint." After the work was done, they gave me a bill for $800 for their labor. They said it took longer than expected, so they decided to bill me! I said no, as expected. **HELL WOULD HAVE TO FREEZE OVER BEFORE I PAY $800! ABSOLUTLEY NOT A CHANCE!**

A few days later, I got a letter from the Tenancy Branch informing me of the date of my hearing regarding the outstanding amount owing of $800. There was no signed agreement in place for this, and I couldn't believe I was about to waste my time at another arbitration meeting.

Chapter 38

Arbitration: Tenants 2, Landlord 0

I couldn't believe I got the same arbitrator again. I couldn't believe I lost again. It didn't matter what I said, because I was doomed from the start. Did I get offered a payment schedule? Heck, no. She told the tenants to take it off the next month's rent.

I was getting disillusioned about the role of the Tenancy Branch. I started to realize that it was their branch, so why should they rule in my favor? I also realized that my tax dollars supported this branch. I got dinged for another $35 for filing fees. I also realized I didn't much care for that arbitrator.

I tried to reflect on the whole process later. I realized I was swimming upstream during the whole thing. I also realized that I had a permanent image implanted in my brain of the tenants and arbitrator with this real smug "I told you so" look on their faces. They were just short of doing high-fives after the ruling. I thought I would try to be philisophical about this whole thing. If a tree falls in the forest, and it lands on their heads but no one else is there to hear it, does it make a sound?

The weather forecast for that day was "normal" throughout the world except for Hell. For some reason **IT HAD FROZEN OVER!**

During the next few days I had the privilege of hearing "So I hear you lost" from the rest of the tenants. Even their kids were giving me the thumbs-down. Didn't matter if I was at the duplex or the fourplex, they all knew about it. I started to think the victorious tenant had placed an ad in the paper.

One tenant said that if he had known I was going to pay $800 to get the place painted, he would have done it for $750. He was actually upset with me that I didn't **check** with him first. "**Check** the temperature in Hell," I told him.

I was definitely in a lose-lose situation here. If I told all the tenants that they were not allowed to do any work on the place, then I could guarantee they wouldn't, and that meant I would get stuck with it. And if I let them do things, they knew I'd get stuck with paying bills big-time. They knew I couldn't predict the weather forecast.

I wore a big "L" for Loser on my forehead for months.

Later that week, something totally stupid happened to me (the big "L" was still attached to my forehead). I was at the gas pumps filling up the old Dodge and fuming about one of my tenants who "just had to see me" at ten o'clock at night. So what did I do? I put diesel fuel in by mistake. I lasted for about two blocks and I pretty well had to beach the car. Naturally, I was halfway between my place and the tenant's, and miles away from a pub. I got in trouble from my girlfriend for getting home late, got heck from the tenant for not showing up, and I had to endure the laughter from the mechanics who flushed out the diesel from my car engine. Oh, and it cost me $150 for the engine flush and $35 for a tow truck, never mind the $40 worth of diesel that I paid good money for to make my car not run.

I'm telling you, one BIG "L" for Loser.

Chapter 39

The Smoke Alarm Works Fine

I got a call at 4:00 in the morning. One of my tenants who didn't speak English very well was yelling at me. I could hear a very loud siren-type noise in the background. I was a little groggy from waking up at 4:00 a.m., but I soon realized that it was the smoke alarm that was going off. I had to hold the phone about a foot from my ear or I would have blown an eardrum.

I couldn't tell if there was a fire or not. He just couldn't get across to me what the problem was. I had no choice: I told him to get out of the building. I phoned the fire department and then all the tenants in the fourplex. Get out of the building! Fire! Run for your lives!

When I got there, all the tenants were gathered outside as two fire trucks pulled up. I suddenly wished I had my rent book because this would have been a perfect opportunity. I should remember this for the next time.

Well, what happened was my tenant decided to have a cigarette at 4:00 in the morning directly under the smoke alarm. It went off and he didn't know how to turn it off. That's why he called me.

I thought to myself, "Why me?"

Chapter 40

Toilets

So I was staring at a plugged toilet. I thought to myself, "Why on Earth am I standing here staring at a plugged toilet with stuff in it that doesn't want to flush away? I just finished dinner and now you're showing me this. Well, why don't you just wrap it up and I'll take it home."

I started thinking. The upstairs suite has two toilets. I'm staring at the one in the basement suite. That means there are three more on the other side, and two more back at my place. That's eight flippin' toilets that all have the ability to demonstrate how the tenant last used them. Marvelous. "Look, Mr. Landlord, here's what I've plugged your toilet up with today. Why don't you reach in to see if you can unplug it?" I wondered if ramming her head down the toilet would help to unclog it.

Toilets are not limited to simply plugging up. No, they break, leak and overflow, just for starters. Toilets even know how to sweat. Apparently there's no caulking too strong and no linoleum too thick for a toilet to do its nasty work on. Add it to the fact that your average male only shoots at the ninety percent level and doesn't feel required to clean up after himself.

I would like to meet the person who first figured out that all the moving parts of the toilet could be made of metal. If the parts are not already submerged in water, then the rest are being misted every morning from a hot shower. I believe that idea alone caused the creation of the Parts Department that I frequent on a weekly basis.

I had to replace an entire bathroom floor once because a toilet managed to leak into the floorboards. The leak that the toilet created was so good that it managed to soak up into the walls as well. I mean, I might as well replace the walls while I'm at it, right?

I made sure that everybody had a plunger. Unfortunately, plungers don't come with a set of instructions, so they were hardly ever used. Tenants have a habit of taking the plungers with them when they leave.

I guess they look at it as my little thank-you gift for all the fun times we had.

Chapter 41

It Happened So Fast

A significant thing happened to me one day. I got married. I held out for thirty-six years as a bachelor, but finally it happened. I guess it was love, but what I really remember was that she said she would help me take care of the properties.

At first, being married didn't change much of anything. All the guys would come over to watch football all day Sunday and again Monday night. I was in three different football pools, so I had to watch all the games. It was pretty well a standard guy thing that there were no rules for watching football. (Football already had enough rules.) As a matter of fact, it was a good excuse to break the common rules of etiquette. The guys were good at that.

Well, the next thing you know, we got introduced to "finger foods." We had never eaten anything off a platter before. Our food groups came from cardboard boxes and easy-to-open bags. It was great for a while, but partway through the season that all stopped. Actually, now that I think about it, that was my last football season with the guys.

Anyway, there was lots to do around the house. Suddenly, things like sawing boards on the kitchen counter were "not appropriate." I thought that, up to now, it was macho, but apparently I was wrong. I couldn't possibly think of revealing my laundry habits to you, except to say that I was saving a bundle on detergent, and I didn't even know it. That habit died a real quick and painful death.

There were other things, too. I couldn't store all of my sports stuff in the living room anymore. We had to buy dishes and salt and pepper shakers, and no more multi-dimensionally cooked steaks.

They had to be medium rare now. Only one case of beer in the fridge at a time so we could have room for "vegetables." My freezer had seen the last of the Ice Age, and I had to move my pet glacier (named Frigid) out of it. Frigid was perfectly trained to hold one warm beer in the center of the freezer, thereby encasing it in ice. All you had to do was set the timer for four minutes and, bingo, cold beer. I was afraid I was seeing the last of my Neanderthal days, and I was obviously moving up into the next stage of evolution: the Dark Ages. But at least I had the comfort of knowing I was evolving.

One other point of interest was the condition of the house when guests were scheduled to arrive. Apparently there was more to it than just having beer in the fridge. That's when I got introduced to such things as vacuum cleaners, clean towels and salad bowls. I'll tell you, someone made a killing when they got away with pawning off salad bowls as being a necessity. Plus, I had to go to the kitchen if someone wanted something. "What's the matter, your legs broken?" was now considered to be an inappropriate response to our guests.

I think I know how the whole thing happened, too. It started when she left her hairbrush in my bathroom. I'm telling you guys, that's how it happens; so listen up, because soon after that her favorite towel moved in. The key here is that they don't make an effort to correct this "oversight." The items just stay. Soon after that a casserole dish wound up in my cupboard, followed by some fashion magazines on my coffee table. Now you've got to realize that it might not happen in this order, but the second you see the hair conditioner move into the shower stall, trust me, that's her way of giving you one week's notice that she's moving in. When that happens, you might as well give her the access number of your ATM card and get it over with.

Oh, and another thing, they never touch your beer during the **Pagan Relocation Ritual**. Somehow that's one of the rites of passage or something like that, but trust me, that sure changes real quick.

If I can save just one guy's soul with this information, then I'm happy and I've done my job. Don't forget, look for the hairbrush and run from the conditioner. I can't make it any clearer than that.

Oh yeah, they call her Bev.

Chapter 42

Simply Amazing

Not too many things amaze me anymore. Not since I've been married, anyway. But tenants are simply in a category all to themselves. It is best described as an ongoing state of euphoria. I mean, why not? Think about it. "Here, Mr. Landlord, here's a $450 deposit and I get your $175,000 home to use as I see fit." How can they not glow when they can make a deal like that? It's simply amazing.

The other day I just happened to be in the neighborhood. There, being loaded onto the back of a truck, was one of my refrigerators. My tenant was, naturally, helping. I asked, sarcastically, if he needed a hand. "No," he says. "I know what I'm doing."

We sat down to have a discussion. To this day, I still do not believe he understood that if you buy a new fridge for yourself, you don't get to trade **my** fridge in as part of the deal. I had to scratch pictures in the dirt with a stick to show him where his reasoning was flawed. I was lucky. He was planning on updating the washer and dryer next week.

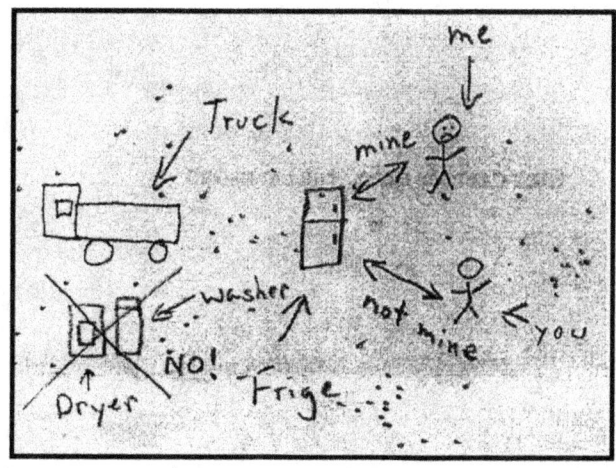

One day I got a call from one of my tenants. She said there was a TV in the front yard surrounded by broken glass from my window. She said it didn't look like the TV was working anymore.

My tenants had thrown their TV out the window. Naturally, it was winter and it was cold. I asked them why they had thrown the TV out the window, and they replied, "It was an accident." They wanted the window fixed right away; it was cold and they were losing heat. They said my insurance should cover the cost of the window as well as the TV.

Now, I'm a reasonable person. Actually, I was a reasonable person with a great big headache. I explained to them about the $50 deductible for the insurance. I explained that they needed insurance for their belongings, like TVs. I explained how my premiums might increase because of the claim. They sat and listened to every word I said. Then they asked if I could try and get them a BIG SCREEN TV as a replacement.

Another topic that deserves mention in the Simply Amazing category has to do with kids' toys. THEY'RE EVERYWHERE! It takes me an hour to cut the lawn. Only half an hour of cutting *per se*, because the first half hour is spent picking up the toys. The thing is, I never see any kids attached to them.

The toys just magically appear overnight. Oh yeah, and just for fun the blessed little things dug a big hole in the backyard and filled it with water. It was their first and last attempt at installing an outdoor swimming pool.

I guess they must see the mean old Landlord drive up in his car, and then that's when they run into the house for shelter. Usually I see their tiny little faces staring out the window at me. Probably the kids are applying the descriptive words that their parents use when they're talking about the Landlord. They've probably never seen a real live monster wandering around in their yard before. Just call me T. Rex.

This one lady tenant was real quiet. She had given me a bunch of postdated cheques when she moved in, and in the four months that she was there I never heard from her. Her cheques never bounced, either. (Probably because they weren't those scenic ones.)

I gave her a call to see if everything was all right. Besides, I wanted to check the water heater I'd installed just before she moved in. So I called her, and another lady answered the phone. I asked to speak to my tenant, and she said she wasn't available and would I like to make an appointment to see her.

"Okay," I said. "How about tomorrow morning?"

She said, "Fine, how about 11:00?" Then she asked me if I'd seen her friend before.

Another strange question, but I said, "Yes, about four months ago."

She said, "Good. Do you want half an hour or a full hour?"

Strange question, I thought, but I told her half an hour was more than enough. "It shouldn't take long to service my little water heater," I told her.

She kind of snickered a bit. Probably because my water heater only held thirty gallons.

When I got there the girl who answered the phone greeted me at the door. She told me to come in and make myself comfortable. She also asked if I wanted a glass of wine. A glass of wine, I thought. At 11:00 in the morning? With all the things I have scheduled to do today? I said, "Sure, sounds good."

A few minutes later my tenant entered the room. She was scantily dressed in some lingerie. She was smiling for a second and then her jaw dropped all the way down to her push-up bra. She looked at her friend and cried out, "That's the Landlord, you idiot!"

Well, good grief. I should have known something was wrong when a tenant offered me a drink. Sure enough, I was the Landlord for an escort agency of some type. Fred's Brothel, I thought. Didn't have a very good ring to it. Not in court, anyway. Well, she cried and begged me not to kick her out. "Heck," I said, "you're the only one who pays the rent on time. You're not going anywhere." It only took a few minutes to check out the water heater. It was fine. I just hoped she wasn't going to charge me for the full half hour.

On another occasion I noticed something simply amazing. It had to do with one very innocent wire going up from one of the basement suites to one of the top suites. That's when I noticed another wire under the eavestrough connecting the two top suites. I went around the corner and there was another wire making its way down to the last suite.

Sure enough, everyone was connected to one cable system for their TVs and stereos. Well, what do you know, I thought. They even have a Secret Handbook for the Cable Networks.

Chapter 43

Sinks

I was staring at a clogged sink. I asked the tenants what they had been thinking. I told them they had a better chance of jamming a rhinoceros down the sink than what they had been trying to get down it. I asked them if they understood the concept of what a sink is supposed to do.

When I left home, my mother insisted that I learn two things. I had to learn how to sew on a button, and how to make a sandwich. She said that I would always be prepared if I knew how to sew on a button and I would never be hungry if I learned how to make a sandwich. I never forgot those lessons. So I was prepared. I had a crescent wrench with me and I was hungry, so I asked the tenant to make me a sandwich.

Now, I had never had any training in "sinkology," but there were bolts to loosen and that was good enough for me. I started adding up how many sinks I had. They had the kitchen one with the two bathroom ones and one in the laundry room. There were two more downstairs. Six more on the other side to make twelve. Add the four from my place and there were sixteen altogether. Looked to me like I had better learn how to fix these little suckers.

I felt like I was under the sink for the better part of the day. I found out you can't drink beer lying on your back. All the blood rushed to my face, and my legs fell asleep on me. All my knuckles on the one hand were a shiny red. Then we decided to put some Drano down the pipe. It cleared up the clog right away. It was as easy as sewing on a button.

Chapter 44

Things Are Still Happening!

My fence fell down. Why it fell down, I don't know. My tenants were standing around it like it was some sort of car accident. I was the ambulance attendant rushing to the scene.

The fence was only wounded. If I did some bypass wood surgery I could save it. I told the tenants that I could use a little help supporting the fence while I worked on it. Within a few seconds they vanished completely. I don't know why things happen the way they do.

One of my tenants left the other day. She just vanished in the middle of the night. She never even asked for her damage deposit back. She was a very nice girl. When I was checking the suite over, I noticed it was very clean. She had left behind a small rug in the middle of the living room. I went to move it over to the entrance where it usually sat. I picked it up and that's when I noticed a ten-inch square piece of wall-to-wall had been cut out by a knife. I lifted up the ten-inch square and underneath, sprayed in red paint, were two words, "Bye Bye." Try explaining that one.

One day I was checking out a suite with one of my tenants who was moving out. When I got to the kitchen I noticed that the faucet was different. I checked the bathroom and those faucets were different too. They were actually cheap fixtures out of a thrift shop. The tenant denied everything.

I tried to turn one of the faucets on and it didn't work. "So, how long have you gone without water?" I asked.

"It must have just happened," they said.

"And I was born yesterday," I replied.

I looked in the mirror to see if I had the word "idiot" written across my forehead. I had no idea what level of the food chain I was dealing with here. There is only one common denominator when it comes to something like this. It's money. I've got your deposit.

One time I happened to be in a tenant's bathroom. I noticed a hole drilled right through the linoleum in the floor. "What's this all about?" I asked. They told me their son made such a mess when having a bath that they decided to make a hole for all the water to drain out. Well, that certainly explained the water stains on the walls downstairs.

Chapter 45

Driveway

The driveway for the fourplex was one big mother. It was the width of two vehicles at the entrance, and then branched into a 'Y' as it went down under two carports. You could fit two cars under each carport, another three behind that, followed by two more. To top it all off, there was gravel parking off to both sides of the entrance that could hold another four vehicles. All in all, you could put thirteen vehicles on the property.

Somehow, the tenants knew this. They had made the same calculations as I had, and they had personally taken on the task of filling each space with a vehicle. Slowly but surely, every month my driveway would inherit another vehicle. I swore the tenants got together for secret meetings to decide whose turn it was next to buy a vehicle.

One day when I was collecting rent, one set of tenants said they didn't have the money. They didn't mind because they were so excited about the new car they had just bought. They had bought it with my rent money. The funny thing is, whenever I went to collect the rent, all the cars would be there but no one answered the door. It was like a game; I knew if they answered the door I would get my rent. No answer, no rent.

Only rarely did I ever see any of the vehicles leave the lot. They would just sit there until one day a tarp would appear over one. That's when the vehicle was officially declared dead. I would then have the privilege as the Landlord of storing their car until they decided to move out.

I decided to call it "Fred's Used Car and Storage Emporium."

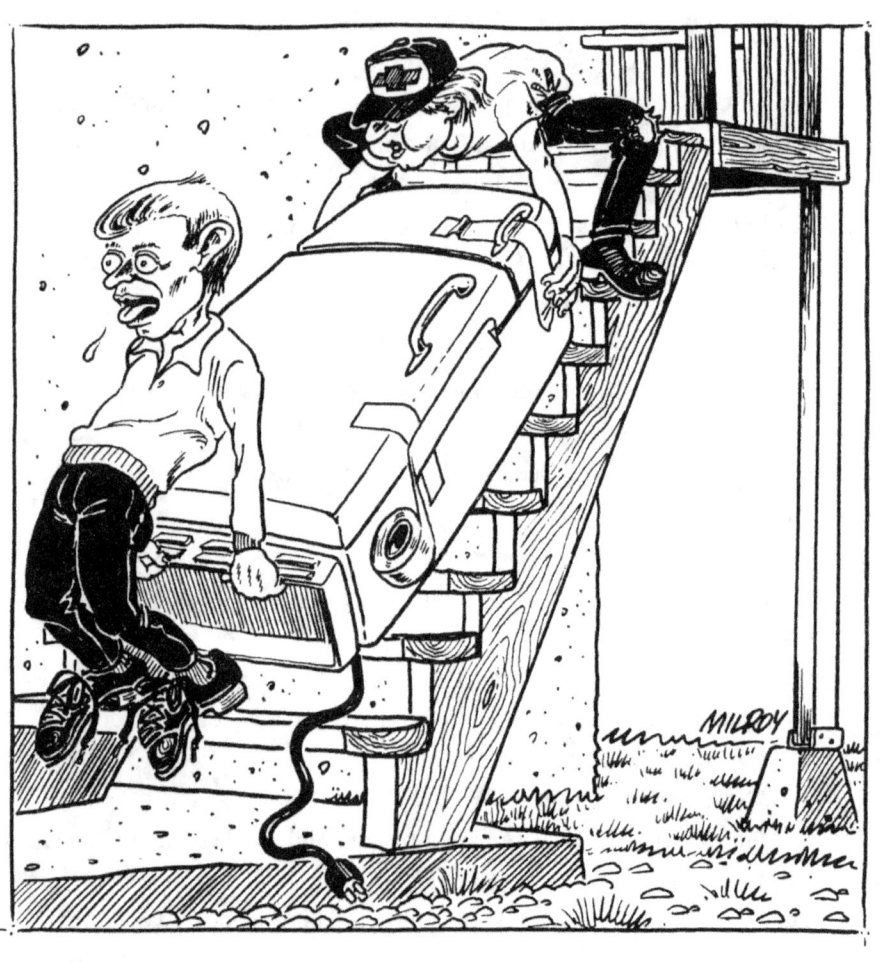

Chapter 46

Illegal Suite? Not Me!

I got a letter from City Hall, from a different department this time. I was really starting to get to know everyone at City Hall. I was surprised they didn't invite me to their annual picnic. This time they wanted to inspect my building because they suspected I might have an illegal suite. Like the thirteen cars out front didn't give it away.

I did some checking around to find out what qualified a suite as illegal. Quite simply, if I had more than one stove and fridge on either side, then I would be deemed as having too many people in a single dwelling residence. Therefore, the suite that had the extra stove and fridge would be illegal.

My plan was simple, yet thought-provoking. I got the building inspector to come over. Dan and I moved the fridge and stove from one suite over to the other. We let the inspector into the top suite and showed him around. He said this is fine, but what about downstairs? We took him down the staircase that connected the two suites. The tenant who lived downstairs was upstairs when the inspector arrived. She just said that this was her bedroom and living area, so what's the problem? Apparently, nothing.

We then went next door. The tenants were all out, as planned. I apologized and said they were supposed to be home, so why don't you come back in an hour? He did. By that time Dan and I had moved all four of the appliances back to the other suite (the original two appliances, plus the two new arrivals). When the inspector arrived, we did exactly the same thing. When he left, Dan and I moved the fridge and stove back to their original suite and we were gone. Got a clean bill of health from City Hall. I suspected my file was getting pretty thick over there.

Dan looked at me funny when this particular event was over, but I told him there were more important things to worry about.

Chapter 47

Garbage

"Not my garbage" was a standard line that came with every tenant. Even if it was on their balcony, I'd hear, "It was there when we moved in." Bottom line, it ended up being my garbage.

I got a letter from City Hall saying that they weren't picking up my garbage anymore. It wasn't properly packaged. I sent them a letter saying garbage is garbage, and you're lucky it's even in a bag. I told them no more Property Taxes until you apologize and pick up my garbage. I think they still remember the lawn mowing episode, because they wouldn't do it.

One of my tenants said they would haul it away for $25. I said sure. A few days later a city inspector showed up at my door with "correspondence" that had my address on it.

"Is this your address?" he asked.

I tried to speak Japanese, but that didn't work. "Yes," I admitted.

"Well, we found this in a whole bunch of trash that was thrown onto the side of the road. We think you did it."

Good grief, I thought. I could have put the garbage on the side of the road myself and saved $25. I knew I hadn't done it, but I knew it was my garbage. I tried speaking French. I still remembered some words from school. I recited three words that described an apple tree. Unfortunately, the inspector was fluent in French. So I confessed and told him the whole story. When he checked it out with the tenant, the tenant said no transaction between the two of us had ever occurred. He actually said, "What garbage?" Thanks a lot.

Later, the tenant told me he was on parole and couldn't get into trouble. He was very sorry and said he owed me one. Yeah right, take a bullet for me sometime. As for City Hall, I got a $150 fine and a $75 clean-up bill.

As for the tenant, what damage deposit?

And it's not just garbage garbage you have to deal with. I've been stuck with couches, tables, cars, bricks, boards, used tires, bikes, broken lawn chairs, BBQs and kitty litter boxes brimming full of surprises. All of them with a combined value of $5.00. They're never left out for me to see when I'm giving back the damage deposit. No, they're left for me to discover later. I'm on an Easter egg hunt every time a tenant leaves.

And who do you think cleans out the stinking garbage pails? Please, don't insult me with the "T" word.

Chapter 48

Rock Walls and Balconies

One day Dan and I decided to upgrade the fourplex. We were going to build two sundecks over each carport, and a rock retaining wall in the front to help landscape the place. Actually, the idea was to supply a nice deck so that we could up the rent in the top suites, and landscape the front so that we could plant trees to hide the two illegal suites.

The idea was to keep costs down and keep labor to a minimum. So we introduced the old "beer and pizza encouragement program" to our tenants. Basically, work for free and we'll keep your tummy happy and your head light.

This model worked with family, but it was only a theory when we first introduced it to our tenants. We found out that, not only can tenants consume their body weight in pizza, they can also make beer disappear into thin air. All this while giving the impression that work is actually being done.

On one occasion, I noticed that a tenant was always going back into his suite every time he opened a beer. When he came out, the beer was always empty. Thirsty worker, I thought. Not so; I found out later that he was filling up a pitcher in his fridge for later.

We got all the rock from a construction site, used sand from a beach, and I still had cement left over from my neighbor. No overhead there. I found a lot where they were starting to build a house. They were just getting ready to clear the land for construction, so I asked the builders if I could dig up the trees that were sitting where the house was going to be built. They said sure. Later on, I came back and borrowed some soil that they didn't want from the hole they dug to put in the basement. It took two weekends and it was done. Looked pretty good, too.

Dan, on the other hand, did the decks. His main goal was not to fall off the deck. Most of the wood we got was leftovers from lumber yards. It was the kind of wood that's warped, with lots of knots in it. Good enough for us, and boy, did we get it cheap. They were happy to get rid of it. Dan finished the decks in two weekends. The total cost for both projects was just under $100 for supplies.

Beer and pizza, on the other hand, cost over $200.

Chapter 49

A Fateful Day

I didn't know whether to be happy or sad. My brother Dan was getting married and wanted to sell the property. He wanted me to buy him out. The sad part was that if I bought his fifty percent share, I'd also be buying the fifty percent of the problems that Dan took care of. The happy part was that Dan was getting married to a very organized type of girl, and Dan's living habits were worse than mine. Marriage would look good on him.

We arrived at a fair market value of $123,000 for his half. That was a healthy profit of $53,000 for him. Naturally, we had to do all the bank and lawyer stuff. Wouldn't want to leave those two food groups out of the profit margin, now would we?

So we went to the bank. The bank manager wanted to know what I was purchasing the other half of the property with. "Absolutely nothing," I said. We all laughed so hard we cried. Here we go again.

Well, they wouldn't give me the money. I told them the heck with you; I've been turned down by better banks than you. I wasn't in the mood to give up. I had the fourplex with one bank and my duplex with the other bank. If I could convince a third bank that I'd give them both mortgages, maybe they would be interested.

I was right. A few days later the bank that had turned me down got my mortgage paid out. They were somewhat miffed because Dan and I had been dealing with them for six years. They sent me a letter stating their concerns. I didn't hesitate to mention the idiot banker who had forced me out of their bank to another one.

My brother continued to do his banking there, though. He found out soon after that the idiot banker got transferred to the most northern branch they had. Looked good on him. It was a sad day for me when everything was finalized. Dan and I had beaten all the warnings we had received about doing business with family. We'd had a great six years together.

I really felt all alone for the first time.

Chapter 50

Here, Kitty, Kitty

One day a little kitten wandered into our place. "Don't feed it," I told Bev, "or it won't go away." Well, it finished my bowl of cereal when I wasn't watching. Ten years later, it still hasn't gone away.

We couldn't decide on a name. I refused to call him Whiskers or Tabby or something sissy like that. Since we couldn't come up with a name, I suggested we just open up the dictionary and point to a name. We did, and it came up "hormone." We laughed at the name but agreed we couldn't call our cat Hormone. Unfortunately, we never did come up with another name, so Hormone stuck. That'll teach it for eating my cereal.

We entered his name in a newspaper contest about weird pet names. Hormone got his fifteen minutes of fame: he came in first. It was just enough for me to let my guard down about my policy of not allowing pets in my rental suites. I rented one unit out to a couple with a cat.

Several days later, the cat had kittens. I swear the kittens had kittens a few weeks after that. There were cats everywhere. I told the tenants that they would have to put some of the kittens up for adoption. They agreed, so who do you think adopted them? The rest of the tenants. The place looked like the SPCA. They had a garbage can dedicated solely to kitty litter.

Unfortunately, cats gets fleas. There's no limit to how many fleas a cat can own. Flea collars just tell the fleas to move to another part of the house and, because the fleas are now bored, they decide to multiply. Fleas multiply every ten seconds. They make their homes anywhere in the house. They don't pay rent and they don't pay attention to eviction notices. Give fleas a chance, and I suspect they could overrun the entire world. It took me three years and about a thousand dollars in extermination bills to finally eliminate the fleas.

And my cat wonders why I look at him funny.

Chapter 51

Doggone It

So did I learn anything from the cat episode? Apparently not. There was now a dog at one of my suites. The tenant just went out and bought one. The rental agreement said no dogs. They knew that; they had signed the agreement.

Okay, I said, no barking and no doggy doo on the lawn. Fat chance. Neighbors called me at three in the morning telling me to shut my dog up. Not my dog, I live two blocks away, and I can't hear it anyway.

There was doggy stuff all over the lawn. "Not from my dog," the tenant said.

"Of course it's from your dog. I never had the problem until your dog got here." What letter do I have on my forehead this time?

I had no choice. The dog went or the tenant did. No way they were going to get rid of the dog, so they got an eviction notice. Two days later I got a letter in the mail informing me of my arbitration date. How could I lose, I thought. It's right there in our signed agreement.

No pets!

Chapter 52

Arbitration: Tenants 3, Landlord 0

Same arbitrator again. Same smirk on her face. Same decision, too.

"Does anyone in your suites have a cat?" she asked.

"Well, yes," I said, "but dogs bark. Dogs make bigger doo-doos on the lawns. I don't want dogs, period, and my tenant agreement states that. Look, they signed right here agreeing to no pets."

"Sorry, Mr. Miller. If the other tenants are allowed cats, then this tenant is allowed a dog."

"What if they bought a rhinoceros?" I asked. "Would that be OK?"

"Now you're being silly, Mr. Miller."

"I'm not zoned for a zoo," I told her.

A couple of weeks later there were two puppies in the next-door suite. Their paws were already as big as a cougar's. They'd probably have to use my rent money to feed them.

Naturally, I got a bill for $35 from the Tenancy Branch. I wrote them back telling them that their ruling had cost me $35 in doggy-doo clean-up fees, and that I would gladly mail them all the doggy-doo as proof of purchase.

I never heard back from them.

Chapter 53

Handyman... Yeah, right

One day one of my tenants didn't have the rent. I mean, he really didn't have the rent. This guy was broke, and I can tell when someone's lying to me. This guy wasn't. We sat down and had a chat and, lo and behold, he told me he was a handyman. So I made him an offer.

My fence back at the duplex needed replacing. My offer was one-and-a-half month's rent to replace the fence, and I'd pay for all the materials. Either that, or he could just leave because this was not a hostel designed for travelers.

He was happy, so we signed an agreement. I didn't want to tax his handyman skills too much, so the deal was to replace my four-foot-high fence exactly the way it was. This would hopefully eliminate any design flaws or miscommunication as to what I wanted. Well, all the materials except the four-by-four posts were delivered. I inspected the load and paid the bill, with the company promising to deliver the four-by-four posts the next day. Unfortunately, my handyman had ordered four-foot-high posts, of which unfortunately, one-and-a-half feet goes into the ground.

You've got it. I came back to see a two-and-a-half foot tall fence–just tall enough to trip over. To add insult to injury, my handyman had a whole bunch of boards left over because I now had a fence that was forty percent smaller than planned. He took them back to the hardware store and got a refund for himself.

Well, I was happy to fill out an eviction notice with a letter stating that he either fixed the problem or I would see him in court. The next day I got a letter from the Tenancy Branch informing me of my arbitration date.

I thought about applying for my own parking spot over there.

Chapter 54

Arbitration: Tenants 4, Landlord 0

I got the same arbitrator again. I produced photos of the fence, receipts from the hardware store, including a copy of the credit the tenant got for the wood I paid for, and I produced the agreement we had on how the fence was supposed to be built. I still lost.

You know what the arbitrator said? "He did his best and since you didn't specify that the posts were to go into the ground, then I can't find him at fault. As far as the credit he received, you will have to take him to court for that, but you can't evict him."

Afterwards, I cornered the arbitrator in the hallway. I was very blunt with my concern that this was the fourth time I had lost. She said something to me that changed my view of fairness forever: "You're the Landlord; you can afford it."

That was the last time I ever showed up at an arbitration hearing. Oh, I've been called to them, but I refuse to recognize them as a form of authority. Besides, it's not my branch.

Chapter 55

Paint

Paint. I've lived a life of paint. All my body parts have been covered with paint at some point in my life. I should have had a paint roller surgically attached to my arm to save time and effort. I don't have "painting clothes." All my clothes are painting clothes. Every time I put on a shirt I get a painting flashback. Whoa, there's suite 607B.

Through all this I still don't know diddly about paint. It took me ten years to realize eggshell wasn't a color, Robertson screwdrivers do not open paint cans, and when a paint can top does finally open, it will land face down on the carpet just inches away from your drop sheet. That's if your lucky! The other option is for the lid to fly off at such a velocity that it sticks to the opposite wall that doesn't need painting. Naturally, it will leave a trail of paint across your face after takeoff.

I've had a million brushes harden overnight. All hair in the suite will attach itself to the freshly painted wall. No matter how much paint you buy, you'll have to go out and buy more. Your paint will not be in stock. When you try to wipe up a painting mistake with a rag, you will end up putting more paint on a different spot with the rag. And it goes on until you get disgusted and throw the rag onto the carpet, and the carpet will spend the night soaking up the paint. And, in the morning, you will have so many bugs stuck on your wall that it will look like a science project.

I've lived a lifetime of paint.

Chapter 56

Moving On

Bev wanted a new house. "What's wrong with this house?" I asked. "It's **your** house. I want **our** house," she said. Like I needed another house.

So we started looking for another house. I had no intention of selling the duplex we lived in. Well, I thought, let's just keep buying up the city until there's nothing left to buy.

Now, so far in my life, I had seen three houses for sale by myself, and I had bought one of them. I saw one with my brother Dan and we bought that one. Using simple math, I had purchased two out of four houses that I had seen. That was fifty percent or, because I played baseball, I liked to think I was batting .500.

Now I was looking at my fiftieth house for sale. I couldn't help but think there was a woman thing in this equation. My batting average was down around .040. From .500. I should have bought twenty-five houses by now. I wasn't getting any further ahead, but I was getting fairly confused.

One place didn't have the right size bathroom. Another one had under-utilized counter space. Now help me here with this one. The toilet worked and there was room for the pizza box on the counter. But apparently I didn't understand, because we just kept on looking.

Finally we found a house. Of course it had an illegal suite. Somehow they're attracted to me. This would bring the total suites to seven. I saw potential in this house: a wall in the kitchen to bash out and attach a sundeck to, and a few other features that needed my type of upgrading.

We closed the deal within twenty-four hours. But I still had to go to the bank for financing because I didn't have any money in the bank. I thought, what the heck, been there, done that, watch me make 'em laugh.

Well, they laughed at the bank all right, but it was a nervous laugh as they handed over the full $120,000 I needed. It seemed that I owed them so much already that they didn't have much choice. Just to make sure I had breathing room with my finances, they also gave me a $25,000 line of credit. I thanked them and asked them very politely not to tell Bev. She would view using up the entire line of credit as a personal challenge.

When I left the bank I did a quick addition in my head to try to figure out what I owed them. It was about $400,000.

Chapter 57

Rent Me!

Now I lay me down to sleep,
Please, oh Lord, just rent my suite.

You have no idea how much of my life I had spent showing suites that were for rent. You sometimes wait around for hours and they don't even show up! The beginning of the landlord-tenant relationship is full of promise and historical facts that don't add up to beans. I watched them unravel in front of my face over the first few weeks.

"Gosh, Mr. Landlord, I love to garden. Can I cut your lawn?" The odds are that they don't know the difference between a lawn mower and a cucumber.

"Gee, Mr. Landlord, I noticed your fence is leaning. I'll fix it for you." Odds are that they'll hit their finger with the hammer and sue you.

"Oh look, Mr. Landlord, your tap is dripping. I'll take care of that for you and I'll check on all the other suites while I'm at it." I knew I had that letter on my forehead again. "Gosh, Mr. Tenant, how much will this REALLY cost me?"

Every prospective tenant has approximately one zillion dollars in the bank. The problem is, they think I have the same amount. They're only interested in renting from me because they were in between buying and selling a new mansion on the water. My place always seems to fall a bit short of their last place. It's not quite as big and doesn't have a view of the entire city. But, for some reason, they want to rent it. Go figure.

As for a reference from their employer or their last Landlord, well, that's hardly a reason for concern. They just happen to be right in the middle of a career change, and the last Landlord has moved to Africa. I liked to tell them that Africa was where I planned to go when they decided to move out one day. It's common knowledge that all Landlords migrate to Africa. During this conversation we all manage to keep a straight face. That's very important because if one of us starts to laugh, we have to start all over again.

The truth of the matter is, I believe that all new landlord-tenant relationships start out with very good intentions. People really do mean well when they promise to pay the rent on time and take good care of the place. The problem being that life in general is taking us down different paths. If the paths were ever to meet, I can assure you that there would be an accident.

Poem to Landlord

Like I'm renting from you,
Took my deposit, you fool.
Gotta think I'm all bent,
If you think you'll see rent.

Maybe you're not all that rad,
And maybe the place ain't so bad.
Just it ain't too high tech,
So forget about that cheque.

Response from Landlord

I'm just not a poet, never claimed to be,
But dang these new tenants, drive me right round a tree.
I'll do everything in my job, even try to be a gent,
Why don't you do yours, and pay the flippin' rent?

One more excuse from that handbook of yours,
You just can't believe how my blood pressure soars.
This ain't no picnic; you don't live on a ranch,
Oops, I forgot; you got the Tenancy Branch!

I think the next advertisement I put in the paper when one of my suites comes up for rent should be more honest. Something like:

Masochist Landlord looking for unemployed sadistic renter to party in his suite. No reference or deposit required. Must be able to pretend to do work around the house for huge sums of money.
Parking spaces available to rent out plus anything not bolted down is considered to be the property of the tenant. Space available on site to open up your own zoo. A Landlord/Tenant agreement must be entered into but it will not be enforced. Paying rent is mandatory, unless it is required to purchase cars, loud stereos, more pets, etc. Suite is available immediately and may be vacated whenever you want, as long as a written, one-hour notice is sent in the mail the day you're vacating (or soon after). Landlord will clean up any garbage left behind and repair all damages left to the suite. Bonus cash awards are available through the Tenancy Branch.

That's probably not what I'll say...but I'm sure that's how they will read it!

Chapter 58

Father's Day

One day I became a father. It was kind of sudden because he came two months earlier than scheduled. The little guy weighed in at three pounds, fourteen ounces. We didn't have a name for him. I felt like calling him Lucky, but that sounded too much like a dog. I thought of going to the dictionary and trying my luck there, but I felt that method was sort of sacred for Hormone.

We called him Sam. One day I would pass my Robertson screwdriver to my son and hang up the rent book. He would take over the family rental business. The sooner he gets old enough to do it, the better.

Over the years Sam became my best friend. He is our only child, so we ended up becoming very close. He took a keen interest in the tenants. Actually, it was the money part that fascinated him. He would arrange all the bills into their denominations and, by the time he was two, he could count past a thousand. The thing was, he was smart enough to figure out that he wanted a piece of the action. An allowance plan was established.

By the time he was three, in his own words he admitted that, *when it came to money, he was an alcoholic!* Pretty big self-analysis for a three-year-old. He was so obsessed with building up his financial equity that there was no job too small for him to do for financial gain.

By the time he was four he was reading his financial statements from his investment portfolio. He had over $1,200 in it. He already had a car picked out for his sixteenth birthday. He assured me that he would take care of me in my old age.

By the time he was six, at the time this book was written, he was a self-confessed money guru. Why? Because he made $200 more in his mutual funds than I did last year, and I have five times the money invested!

You should see the smug look on his face when our financial statements arrive every month.

Chapter 59

My First Workshop

Our new place had a two-door garage and a workshop. I never had a workshop before, so this was exciting. No more cutting boards on the kitchen counter. No more storing old fridges in the living room. I even had a board to hang up all my neighbors' tools. I could finally get organized.

There were two words that were now part of my vocabulary: "haven" and "sanctuary." It all added up to this feeling called "bliss." Unless you've felt it, you can't understand it. Bev just called it a place for me to hide out, but I knew better. I was in tune, and I was finding myself in the garage. Women say we never get in touch with our feelings, but that's not true. I'm sure that's why God created workshops.

I started to fix and build things. That's why you have a workshop, right? I had one area to put the things that needed fixing, and another area for the things that didn't pass the workbench test. In order for an item to fail this test, it had to be uncooperative when trying to be fixed. This particular area expanded over time with a lot of items that I deemed technically inferior.

When I got tired of items always failing the workbench test, I tended to start creating things. Like the wooden stamp holder that I made for the kitchen one day. I thought it was pretty good, but Bev said it was a few boards short of a patent. I ended up hanging it in the garage and storing electrical connectors in it. I had a lot of those because I was too scared to use them. I was still growing back a fingernail from the last time.

Bev even gave me a chance to fix the TV set when it decided not to work one day. I didn't hesitate to make the statement that I had never fixed a TV before, but I was willing to give it a shot. After several days my original statement remained true to form. The repairman apologized for taking so long to fix it, and that's when I realized it was a complicated matter. Then he said, "If someone hadn't been messing around with the insides, I would have gotten it done a lot sooner." Bev reminded me not to quit my day job.

One section of my workshop was designed for lights. I had swag lamps, small chandeliers, outdoor lamps, kitchen lights, and about twenty regular bathroom and bedroom lights. I bought light bulbs in bulk and had about two hundred of them (somehow tenants decide to leave when the last light bulb burns out).

All these lights were hanging from the wooden rafters, and it basically looked like a lighting shop. I had one full cupboard dedicated to light switches, circuit breakers and light switch plates. The funny thing was, there were all these lights hanging around, and the lighting in the workshop wasn't all that good. At least all that stuff was stored off the ground, compared to my carpet and linoleum showcase display at the other end of the workshop.

The great thing about having a workshop is that you lose all concept of time. It's like you fall into some sort of space continuum where reality doesn't exist and the outside world is totally dependent on your pending success. During these prolonged workouts, I've developed the Miller Theory. Not to be confused with Einstein's theory. My theory can be understood and explained.

It's like $E=MC^2$, only in a workshop the "E" stands for Earnings. Simply, I'm there to save the Miller (the "M") household a lot of money by doing things myself. My Earnings are, in a sense, my prime directive. The "2" stands for the option of squaring or doubling the time I spend in the shop, which is critical to the output which, in turn, generates the Earnings. The "C" is a wild card. Every night I "C" if Bev will let me go down to the workshop. I try to convince her that I can do better than the stamp holder.

One day I did produce a masterpiece. Not to be confused with Van Gogh, my particular piece of art was entrenched in a rich burgundy. I was making wine, and my first bottle of wine hit the palate square in the taste buds. Bev thought it was great and I figured my workshop had just gotten a reprieve from the auto wreckers. I had produced my first hit single that made the hit parade, and my shop should stay solvent throughout my tenure.

I was back to bliss and life was good.

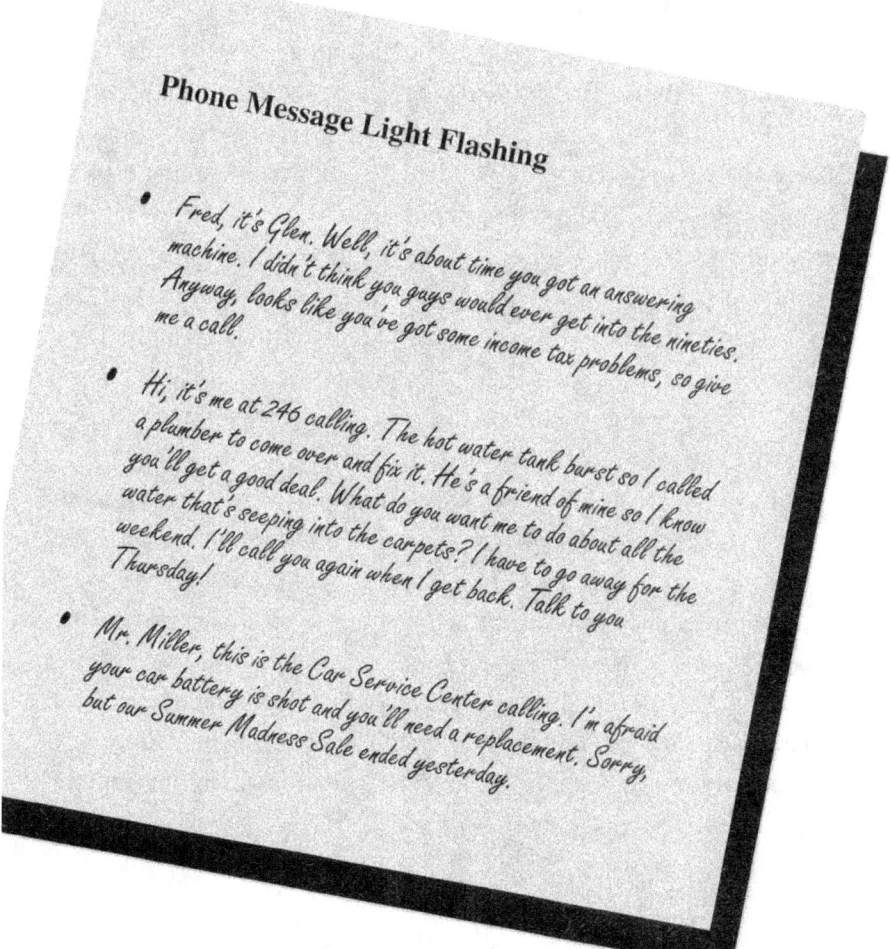

Phone Message Light Flashing

- Fred, it's Glen. Well, it's about time you got an answering machine. I didn't think you guys would ever get into the nineties. Anyway, looks like you've got some income tax problems, so give me a call.

- Hi, it's me at 246 calling. The hot water tank burst so I called a plumber to come over and fix it. He's a friend of mine so I know you'll get a good deal. What do you want me to do about all the water that's seeping into the carpets? I have to go away for the weekend. I'll call you again when I get back. Talk to you Thursday!

- Mr. Miller, this is the Car Service Center calling. I'm afraid your car battery is shot and you'll need a replacement. Sorry, but our Summer Madness Sale ended yesterday.

Chapter 60
Golf

One day I was so frustrated with the whole landlording thing that a friend of mine said I just had to figure out a way to relax. He suggested getting outside and taking up a relaxing sport. He suggested golf. When I got there I bought ten golf balls from some kid who was selling them at the first hole. I thought since these were my friend's borrowed clubs, I'd leave him with a few extra golf balls in appreciation. Beats me where this kid got so many golf balls.

Since I didn't know a good golf ball from a bad one, I just went with color groups. By the time I'd finished the first hole, my friend said I had the biggest slice he'd ever seen. I just called it going all the way over to the right. I figured this big slice was coming back to haunt me for always grabbing the biggest slice of pizza when the box opened. This "big slice" became my feature shot which I could always depend on, even when putting. Anyway, the course was designed to have all the fairways and greens on the left and all the sand traps, water hazards and out-of-bounds on the right. It played right into my game. "Oh look, another dogleg left. Wonder which way my ball will go?"

I met up with the ball-hawk kid again when we finished the ninth hole. I had calculated my holes-per-ball ratio, and realized I needed eight more balls in order to finish the game. I got ten just to be on the safe side. The kid asked me if it was OK to follow me around the last nine holes. "No big deal," I said.

I found a different level of frustration that day. What got me was that I had paid a lot of money to find this new feeling of anxiety. My friend told me to relax and swing the club. How can you do that when you want to kill the flippin' ball and destroy your clubs?

I didn't throw the bag of clubs into the water to join my balls because (1) they weren't my clubs, and (2) there were still three beers left in the golf bag. I teed up on the eighteenth, silently vowing that I would never do this to myself again. While positioning the ball, I noticed a big gash on its cover. I stared at it and realized it was the same smirky smile I'd seen several times on the face of that stupid arbitrator at the Tenancy Branch. I hit the ball so hard it flew into another time zone.

God, I love that game!

Chapter 61

Workshop Maneuvers

I got a free table for my kitchen one day. Two of the legs were wobbly, but hey, I had a workshop. Put the thing on the workbench and replaced all the screws on the legs to make sure they were solidly fastened to the tabletop. Unfortunately, the screws were half an inch longer than the thickness of the table, so all the sharp ends were pointing up through the tabletop.

Now, I could have just taken the screws out, but that would have left me with twelve holes on the tabletop. I sat and stared at my stupidity for a while. Some song was playing in the background about some guy coasting down the highway. I thought, why not? I got four coasters made out of cork and banged them on top of the screws. Naturally, they were perfectly proportioned.

"Look, honey, I fixed it so the table has built-in coasters."

"What a good idea, dear."

Sold it to a tenant a week later for $75. Gotta love me!

I noticed over time that I didn't have much room in my workshop with all the flippin' appliances stored in there. There were two fridges, two stoves, two washing machines and one dryer. I don't even remember how they got there, but it was time to get rid of them. I had a pile of paint supplies scattered everywhere, and I needed that space. Besides these seven appliances, with the eight in this house added to the other thirty, the total came to forty-five. Time to scale down

So I remembered a friend of mine was having a garage sale. I asked him if he would mind if I brought the appliances over for him to sell for me. No problem. I tried to get my tenant to help me with loading the appliances onto a truck I had borrowed. He wasn't home. Had to make three trips and I did it all myself.

At the end of the day my friend called with good news/bad news. You sold three appliances; come on by and get your money and pick up the other four. Again, my tenant wasn't around to give me a hand. Two trips later, I got the four appliances stored back in, you guessed it, the workshop. The fridge, stove and washer were still at my friend's house with a sold sticker on them. The people who bought them were arranging for a truck to pick them up later.

I thought I would grab a quick sandwich before I returned the truck. I was in the kitchen when my tenant knocked on the door. He looked pretty happy. "Can I ask a favor of you?" he asked.

"Depends what it is," I replied.

"I just bought three appliances at a garage sale and I was hoping you would help me pick them up and let me store them in your workshop. I see you have a truck out there."

I'll bet you Las Vegas wouldn't even put odds on this one happening.

So I stored my paint in his fridge and stove. All the paintbrushes and rollers went in the crisper and the paint trays went in the freezer. The washing machine stored all my drop sheets, and I used the lint trap to store my color card samples.

There went a whole flippin' Sunday down the tubes, my back was killing me, and I still didn't have any room in my workshop.

Chapter 62

Exercise

All my friends were now going to health spas. Exercise was the in thing. I never had the time, nor did I have a pair of shorts that didn't have a hole in them. I was too busy bench pressing water tanks into place and pumping appliances. I had three lawns to cut and a clogged gutter to get to that day. I didn't know what pecs were until someone pointed at mine and said I had big ones.

"Where do you work out?" they asked.

"At the gym for Landlords," I replied. "It's free and it's open twenty-four hours a day."

I didn't have the time to compare body parts. I had one more lawn to cut, and I only had one more health juice left from my six-pack.

I don't mind getting my hands dirty but, to be honest, I would just as soon watch someone else do the grunt work. I was at the up-and-down duplex one day. These two guys were halfway up the stairs hauling a large fridge, so I asked them if I could help. Both of them looked at me with sweaty faces and one said, "Do you live here?" It was said in a not too friendly tone, so I answered honestly, "No." They both glared at me for having the gall to interrupt their work.

I got to watch them hauling that fridge up one step at a time for about another ten minutes. I didn't have anything else to do at the moment, because I also had to get to the top suite, and I couldn't get past them on the stairs. When they finally did get to the top, they knocked on the door and my tenant answered. We all stood there looking at her. The two men were pleased to announce that her new fridge had arrived. My tenant looked puzzled and said, "Fred, you know that fridge is for downstairs." The two men glared at me and all I could say was, "Hey, don't look at me. I don't live here!"

With exercise, there's also the health side of things. The good news is I never get sick enough to go to a doctor. The bad news is that doesn't leave any excuses not to do the Landlord thing.

I saw my doctor one day because my Mom said I had to get my cholesterol checked. There must be a million things available for a doctor to check, but my Mom picked cholesterol, so that's what I was there for.

The first thing my doctor said was, "I haven't seen you for twelve years. I figured you were dead."

"Sort of," I replied. "I'm a Landlord now."

She said we should do a complete physical some time. I told her I was married, but thanks anyway.

When I got the cholesterol results I rounded the number down so I could remember it, and then gave it to my Mom. I guess I passed, because Mom then made my brother Dan go to the doctor for the same thing. Apparently Dan didn't beat my score; now he has to report his food intake to Mom all the time to help his cholesterol score. Mom said that he should phone me and "Try and eat more like your older brother."

I gave Dan the number of my favorite pizza joint.

Chapter 63

Real Estate

Over the years I watched the real estate market with a vested interest. The market was literally booming. We baby boomers were doing it.

Every month the newspaper showed statistics on housing values for the month. It also did a cost comparison over the years. Houses were going up $20,000 a year. Most people thought they were making money. The reality was that when they sold, it would just cost them more to buy another house, so they technically were not any further ahead. I, on the other hand, liked my position. I had no money in the bank, but I sure looked good on paper!

I wrote up my first financial statement, but I didn't really know what I was doing. I felt that if I did a financial statement, I would seem more important. It looked like the illustration on the left.

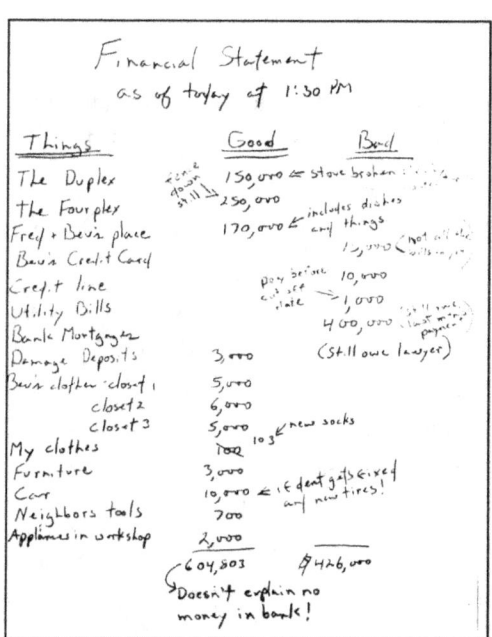

This was my first and last financial statement. There was really no point in doing another one. It was way more fun playing with Sam.

Chapter 64

Income Tax Maneuvers

I tried to do my own income tax. I didn't understand the English version, so I switched to the French side of the form. It was a bit better because I got a few more fields filled out on the French than on the English side. I figured it was not too bad for someone who only knew the French names for all the parts of an apple tree from grade six. I also knew one to five in French. Or "oon to sank," as they say.

I looked for a decoding book to help me transform "Revenuespeak" into "Peoplespeak." I even tried blanking out every second word in the instructions to see if there was some kind of secret pattern I was missing. In the end, I used a form of telepathy to guess what it was they were trying to ask me.

When I finished, I didn't like the amount I owed so I did it over again. This time I tried more of a free-form method using random triple-digit numbers. I figured if they can be vague, so can I. I was starting to understand the process. When I finally got the total to equal the amount I owed on my credit cards, I signed it and mailed it in.

My income tax form got rejected. They said they didn't understand my return. That was okay, because I didn't understand what they sent me, so I figured we were both at fault. Well, naive me, Revenue Canada is never at fault. It doesn't matter that they're as confused as I am as to what their rules mean, it's up to me to convince them how they apply to my pathetic little life.

They said I had to come in to their office. I had to bring my records.

I swear I saw them coming out of their offices holding darts in their hands. You see, I figured there was this giant money dartboard in each office. They throw the darts against it to figure out how much you have to pay. They seemed happy because I guess they scored some good numbers with the darts.

I told them I didn't like the score they shot and that I wanted them to go back and do it again. They said they would but, if they did that, then they would want to shoot darts at my last seven years of income tax returns to get new totals. I asked them if they were good shots and they assured me that, not only was the board real big, but they would stand extra close just for me. I asked them if it was okay to write a cheque. They said sure. I actually walked out of the office feeling pretty lucky.

Revenue Canada got a taste of me that day. I could tell they liked how I tasted. I was young and in my prime. There was no fat on my body and I'd look good on their giant BBQ. I was Grade A chow in their eyes and I was slowly marinating, at the same time being beaten just enough to tenderize the meat for the feast. Oh sure, I was small-time game, but I'd make a great appetizer.

They yanked the $100,000 capital gains exemption from everyone. Everyone blamed the decision on me. It was bang, make your declaration now, you low-life peons. Then we're going to round you all up and audit your body parts.

I got an accountant to fill out the new forms. One year later I found out that Revenue Canada did not like the way the forms were filled out. They said I could reapply for the $100,000 exemption, but I would have to pay a penalty. The penalty was one-third of a percent per month on the $100,000. They wanted $4,000 just to fill out the same form again. Beer alone would not kill the pain. I went to Scotch.

ODE TO REVENUE CANADA

There is nothing on Earth more powerful than thee,
Not mountains nor oceans, there's nothing you see.
You can do what you want and then make up the rest,
We'll just duck and take cover and hope for the best.

It's futile to struggle against the laws you impose,
Your army of auditors is the mightiest of foes.
The strength of their character is not the main key,
It's that spot in their hearts where a soul used to be.

I'll open my books and you can sort through my trash,
Take my firstborn, take all of my cash.
Please leave us some food, and maybe one beer,
We should do this again, I'll see you next year.

Chapter 65

Inside Looking Out

I went to a dance with my wife. I figured out a long time ago that there are only two types of people at a dance: the ones who want to watch, and the ones who want to perform. I prefer performing. I'm not saying it's a pretty sight, but every so often I needed the Rolling Stones to help me shake my nerve endings clean. Somewhere inside me was a real person who wasn't a Landlord, someone who was truly warm and compassionate. I felt that suppressed person many times as he screamed to come out, but whenever I let him out he would get crushed almost every time by the system. The system was commonly referred to as "Them." Arbitration, City Hall, Revenue Canada, Banks and yes, tenants. Can't live with tenants, can't live without them, bless their little hearts.

Technically, it's up to Them to make sure the process doesn't seem too easy. If being a Landlord brought fame and riches, everyone would do it. So, it's up to Them to make sure that doesn't happen. It's not a complicated process for Them; instead it's a long slow process, like something decomposing. You don't notice it until it starts to smell bad.

Being a Landlord is **not** a power trip. Actually, it's the opposite. It's like the Prime Minister: he's at the top of the organization charts, all right, but he's totally responsible for and accountable to everyone else (Them). If the people complain, he has to answer for it. Same as a Landlord: if any of Them point a finger, the Landlord answers for it.

If you think for one second that this is a power trip, then go straight to the chapter on **Wacko Land**. Read that and then come straight back to the beginning of this chapter. Repeat if necessary.

I truly believe there's a universal law that allows certain windows in some sort of time continuum to allow Them in at certain times. The law doesn't allow Them to gang up on me all at once, but instead ensures a steady flow. It's like a long line at Disneyland where everybody is anxious to ride *The Landlord*.

I always figured if there was ever to be a fun ride to look forward to it would be a ride on *The Landlord*. There would only be two types of people to ride *The Landlord*: tenants, who are the only ones who pay; and then the rest of Them, the ones who don't pay. Because the tenants pay, they get to ride *The Landlord* twenty-four hours a day. The rest of Them usually only ride during daylight hours.

The funny thing about this ride is that *The Landlord* gets to make the rules before everyone gets on, but once everyone is seated and ready to go, they get to change all the rules. That's just the way it is.

There are no typical rides on *The Landlord*. They're all different. That's probably why everyone keeps coming back for another ride. One thing I noticed was whenever a tenant finished a ride, you had to check to see if anything was broken. As opposed to Revenue Canada, where you have to check to see what's missing. The rest of Them actually have the gall to bill me for the time they spent on the ride.

I wish there was an easy way to describe a ride on *The Landlord*. Ask anyone who's been there, done that, and they'll have a difficult time, too. Try to picture a roller coaster. I mean a giant roller coaster. Now picture the roller coaster over a large bed of molten lava with an intense lightning storm headed your way. Hold that thought.

Now think about it. Do you really want to be a Landlord and go for a ride?

Chapter 66

Fred's Brewery

My home brew beer was flat yet frothy. It was like it climaxed the second you opened the bottle. Some caps just popped off in your hand, and these weren't twist tops. I figured I'd read up on the instructions for the next batch I made.

Somehow, I figured brewing your own beer would end up with some kind of big party with girls in bikinis dancing on the workbench and celebrating some sort of pagan ritual. But there I was with my beer foaming all over the floor, leaving me with nothing but beer bubbles to suck up. I figured it couldn't get much worse than this.

Well, there was still enough light left in the day for me to pull off (another) idiot move. I managed to install a new door lock on one of the suites without hurting myself but, when it came time for testing, I somehow managed to snap the key off in the lock. I couldn't get the broken part out and neither could the people at the hardware store. It seemed that within minutes everyone was talking about the idiot who snapped the key off in the lock. It was almost like they were swarming me to see what an idiot looked like.

Apparently I'll always have more room in my life to fit other stupid things in, and that's why I don't consider myself to be a *complete idiot* just yet. The key here is to try not to look too astonished if I ever do get something done right, or else I'll give myself away.

My wife called me from the house. One of my tenants was mad about something and wanted me to come over to his place right away. I figured I'd pick up a six-pack of real beer on the way.

Chapter 67

Basketball, Insurance and RIP

I set up a basketball hoop on the front of my carport. I thought it would be good therapy and would let me work out my stress. I was into my fourth shot when I decided I was good enough to do a slam dunk with both hands while letting out some sort of primal scream. Like it was the winning basket in game seven of the NBA finals.

The scream came out fine, but I missed the entire net and bounced the ball through the only window in the carport. All the neighbors and their kids came out and stared at me. Bev shook her head as she looked out the window. My basketball career had come to an abrupt end.

It didn't bother me too much that I had to replace the window, because it had a big crack in it anyway. That had happened the month before when I banged the end of the broom handle into it. In any event, it should be the same $50 deductible I'd had to pay the insurance company the week before when I broke the basement window with the ax head that flew off the handle.

Bev came out to inspect the damage and tell me that a tenant was on his way over to see me. "He was really mad," she said. The conversation with the tenant went something like this:

"You promised me you would fix the stove."

"Right after I get the rent you owe me."

"We told you we would have it next week."

"Then that's when your stove will get fixed. Where do you think the money comes from to fix these things?"

Little did they know it, but they were in my new **Rent Incentive Program** (or **RIP**, as I called it). I like to think it had replaced the

Tenancy Branch. This program was controlled by the fuse box and was a lot cheaper than the Tenancy Branch.

"But what will we do until then?"

"I have some great recipes from my bachelor days that don't require any power at all. You should keep these in mind when your fridge, I mean *if* your fridge, goes next week. Best place to store these babies is in your Tenants' Secret Handbook."

I never did have to power down the fridge. The new **RIP** program turned out to be very successful over the coming years.

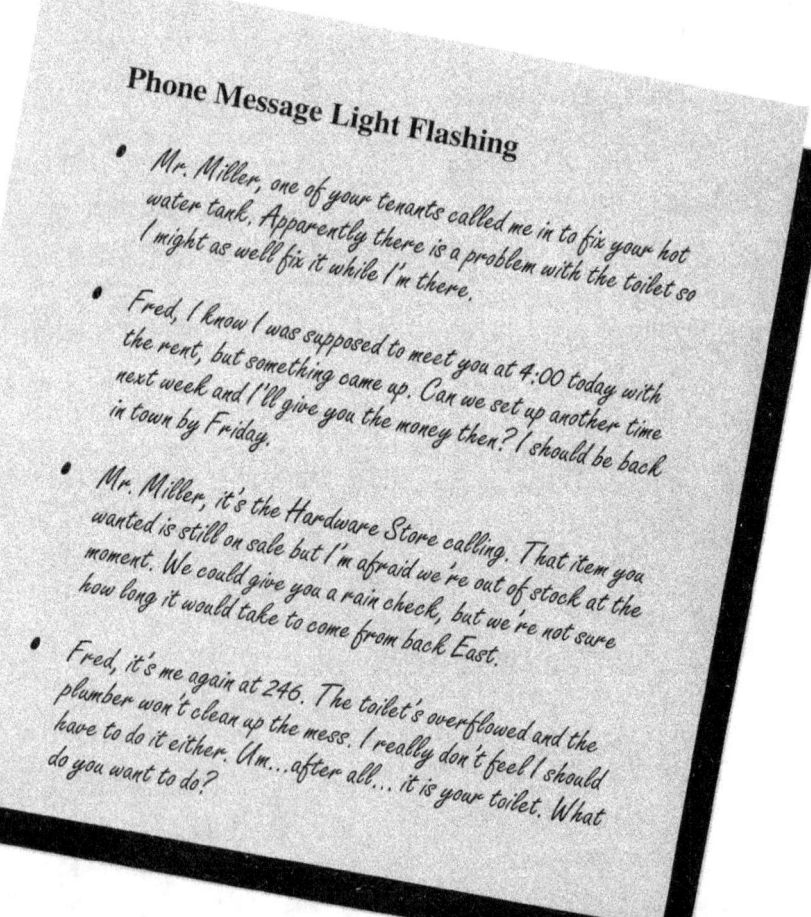

Phone Message Light Flashing

- Mr. Miller, one of your tenants called me in to fix your hot water tank. Apparently there is a problem with the toilet so I might as well fix it while I'm there.

- Fred, I know I was supposed to meet you at 4:00 today with the rent, but something came up. Can we set up another time next week and I'll give you the money then? I should be back in town by Friday.

- Mr. Miller, it's the Hardware Store calling. That item you wanted is still on sale but I'm afraid we're out of stock at the moment. We could give you a rain check, but we're not sure how long it would take to come from back East.

- Fred, it's me again at 246. The toilet's overflowed and the plumber won't clean up the mess. I really don't feel I should have to do it either. Um...after all... it is your toilet. What do you want to do?

Chapter 68

Mind Set

I sat and watched the cat one morning while I was in bed. Why couldn't I be as relaxed as the cat, I thought. Sure, I was on my fourth cup of java, but that wasn't the point. Somehow there should have been a metaphysical, Buddha-type way to transcend myself into a state of euphoria. I just had to take the time to reach out and find the path of contentment. Be one with myself, I thought. Find and open the door to bliss and happiness.

Bev said a tenant and some of his friends were at the door. She told me to get them off the porch before all their weight collapsed it. I didn't feel like I was about to open up the door to bliss and harmony. I believe in what matters. The question is, what matters? What's "real" is what should be considered as to what matters, but not everything is "real." I'm sure that matters to someone else. No matter to me.

The tenant at the door mattered because he was there, and he knew I was here. We would soon be having a conversation that apparently mattered. What kind I didn't know, but it mattered to them and affected me. It seemed to matter to him, but was it real enough to matter to me? It was taking up my time, so that mattered. Time to stop daydreaming and open the door to see what's the matter this time. The conversation went like this:

"What's this letter from you saying I have to move all my car parts off the lawn?"

"I told you it was OK if you were going to fix up your vehicle, but I didn't say you could take the whole thing apart and put it together from scratch."

"Well, where do you want me to put them?"

"Back on the car would be a good place. Right now, half my lawn is brown from you leaving the car parts on it. Another portion is black from all the oil and grease on it, and the rest of the lawn is blue from your paint job. When did you start thinking it was a body shop you were renting?"

The problem with this kind of thing is, as soon as one tenant sees another tenant doing something, they somehow figure they have the green light to do it, too.

"Why did you lend out my lawn mower to your friend?"

"Because the tenant next door loaned it to his friend last week, so I thought it would be OK."

"Why are you putting garbage under the stairs? No, don't tell me."

I thought I'd go with the "laugh and the whole world laughs at you" theory on this one. Stupid cat just doesn't know what's going on, that's his problem.

Chapter 69

Just Another Day

I had to show a suite, and I had a pimple on the end of my nose. I hate that. Puts me in a bad mood. I was the reindeer at the front of Santa's sleigh.

I showed up at the suite and I couldn't even pull into the driveway. There were so many cars and tarps that it looked like a circus had just rolled into town. I gave my "Hail Mary, full of grace, help me find a parking space" to no avail. I parked down the street.

Now, you have to realize that I'm a reasonable guy. I only ask for the basics in life. When the tenants pay their rent, I don't go around snooping and checking up on them. I figured someone should have a life. It might as well be them. So I knocked on the door of the tenant who was going to vacate so I could let the prospective tenants in to see the suite. Lo and behold, they had turned the living room into some sort of shantytown. There were five beds all set up, surrounded by barriers. I was too stunned to say anything. When I looked back to apologize to the prospective tenants, they were already gone.

The kitchen was unbelievable. There was one large pot that spanned two burners. It was surrounded by fifty empty macaroni boxes. The pot had a coating at least an inch thick of pasta that had slowly adhered to it over time. They just kept on using it over and over, without ever washing it. I didn't have the stomach to check out the bathroom.

It would be impossible to rent this suite. They assured me it would be clean, but I knew the only way it was ever going to be clean again would be to torch the place and start all over again. I stopped the ad in the paper and stopped showing the suite. I took a one-month loss and took some time off to clean up the suite and renovate.

The first of the month came and I went in. My anxiety level was at maximum. I held my breath as I looked around. The suite was in perfect shape. It almost sparkled. I rented it the next day.

Actually, I rented it to some "cool kids," as they referred to themselves. Cool kids have to live somewhere, right? So they're cool and I'm not, and apparently the English program at the schools had changed a lot, because I didn't understand some of the things they were saying. I guess the English program switched over to the metric system or something.

So here's kind of how the conversation took place. My interpretation of what I think was transpiring appears in brackets:

"Rad space, Lord man. Looks like you're a cool dude and wicked Lord." (Okay, I know cool and I guess rad is short for radiant, but I'm not sure why I'm wicked and being mistaken for a prominent religious figure.)

"Me and Spaz like split the depot and payouts plus mount the Tillitee man." (Now, this one I think I got. He and Spaz will split the deposit and rent, plus pay the utilities. They were both reaching for their wallets, so I know I was real close with this one.)

The other guy, who referred to himself as Gummy, gestured towards their car and said, "The carma doesn't convert when we hobo the Sure Guy." (Now, this one was a bit harder, but my guess was that they had no money (hobos) for the insurance man (Sure Guy) to keep their car (carma) on the road (convert). I was starting to feel cool.)

This sentenced was followed by: "Pancaked at sunrise and deposed." (So I was either right that their insurance was running out on their car, as in falling flat as a pancake, and I would soon be storing it, OR they were indeed having pancakes at the depot in the morning.)

This last one I figured out about a month after they moved in. "Scaping is for real and we're veggies." (I just figured they liked to escape (scaping) life's little problems by doing drugs and that they liked being "vegged out." We even used that term when I was in high school. But what I found out later was that they were into gardening (scaping or landscaping) and they were vegetarians.)

Spaz and Gummy stayed for about five months. Just long enough to harvest their carrots and lettuce. Nice kids, but a real wicked language.

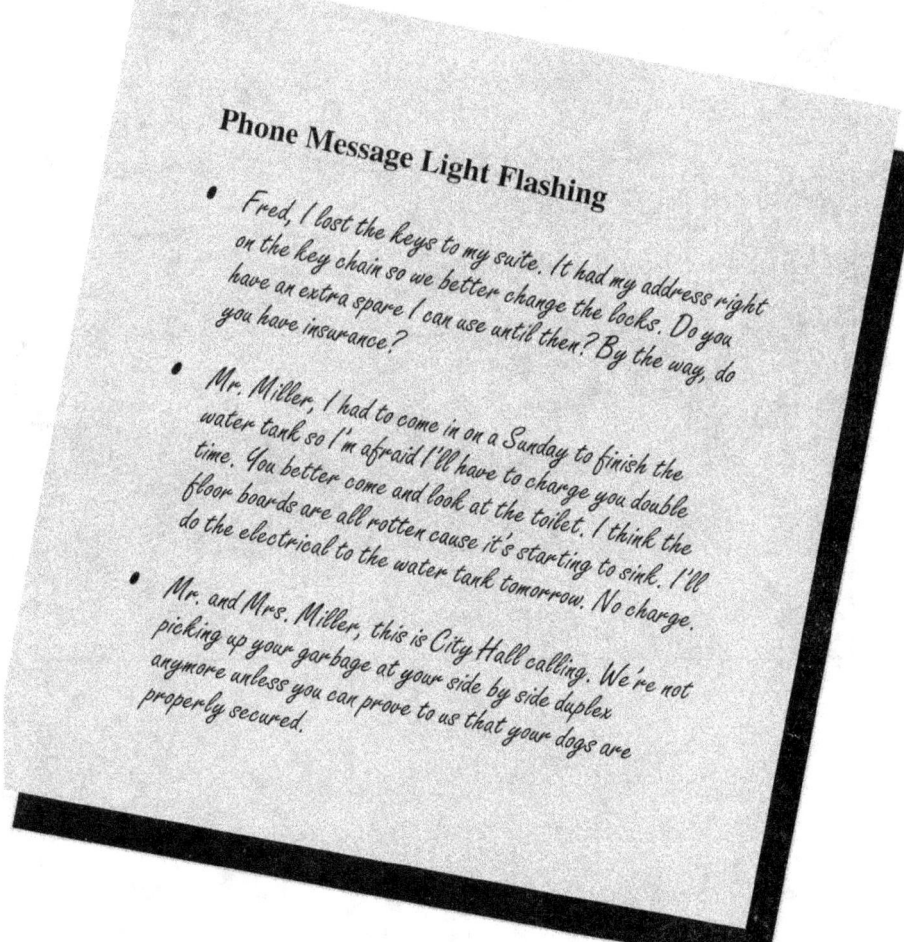

Phone Message Light Flashing

- Fred, I lost the keys to my suite. It had my address right on the key chain so we better change the locks. Do you have an extra spare I can use until then? By the way, do you have insurance?

- Mr. Miller, I had to come in on a Sunday to finish the water tank so I'm afraid I'll have to charge you double time. You better come and look at the toilet, I think the floor boards are all rotten cause it's starting to sink. I'll do the electrical to the water tank tomorrow. No charge.

- Mr. and Mrs. Miller, this is City Hall calling. We're not picking up your garbage at your side by side duplex anymore unless you can prove to us that your dogs are properly secured.

Chapter 70

Dust Bunnies

There was one tenant I couldn't quite read. I like to categorize people, and he was somewhere between a lawn ornament and a fashion accessory. Since I couldn't put my finger on it, I put him under my "Dust Bunny" category.

You see, you have to be able to read people in just about all walks of life. If you don't, most things in your little universe will start to collapse, and you have to go to your doctor for pills that will shift you to a parallel universe. I prefer to stay in my own little universe with all its time warps. At least they're familiar time warps.

The Dust Bunny category, or DB for short, isn't a bad thing. Compared to the Space Cadets and Professionals, the DBs are nothing. I mean that.

Everyone has met a Space Cadet. They're the ones who went into orbit without NASA approval or the requisite training to go with it. They're just on the verge of being permanent time travelers. You have no idea where they are or where they're coming from. Most of the time I don't care. Just give me the rent, and catch you later, rocket man.

The Professionals, on the other hand, are better than me. Not because I think so. No, it's because they tell me they are. I am just a small step (to step on) on their way to fame and glory. Their noses point closer to the sky than mine does, and they're usually "one with the universe." Some of them border on the Space Cadets. With these people I must endure a different level of tolerance. I just show them amazement and astonishment at their level of accomplishment, which I have yet to realize. Usually, this type of person stays the longest at my suites. Go figure.

There are other categories that are fun to slot people into. You all know the Handyman Series, so I won't bother you with that one. But have you ever heard of the Spinners or the Ventilators?

Neither of these categories is easy to spot until it's too late. The Spinners are a touch on the spinny (airhead) side, but the worst part is the spinning of tales. Apparently their real life is lackluster enough for me to get the new and improved version of their daily activities. For some reason they go out of their way to convince me of their saintly status. I have no idea why they're trying to impress me. I don't give a hoot.

The Ventilators are the worst. They talk, talk, talk, talk, talk! Anytime, anyplace, anywhere. I have no idea what they talk about, because my hearing system is programmed to shut off if someone can't get to the point in less than a minute. I've had some of my best daydreams while listening to a Ventilator's monologue.

Getting back to this guy I had to put in the Dust Bunny category. The Dust Bunny category is simple. You don't have to deal with it right away but, if you wait too long, one day you will discover that you have a problem that must be dealt with. Hopefully, you discover it before it mutates. This one mutated. It reminded me of that sandwich I found in my golf bag from last year. It had transformed itself into a brand new food group. Neither the Dust Bunny nor the sandwich came with a warning label.

This DB started sending letters to all the tenants giving them instructions "on behalf of the Landlord." Somehow Mr. DB was running the show now, and was actually "scheduling monthly inspections" of the suites. To tell you the truth, I could have lived with that part of it, except I had this vision of a Supreme Court Judge awarding him $150,000 in back pay for his efforts. "He's your employee," the Judge will tell me. All the phone calls from the tenants asking me why I hired this jerk were enough to put a stop to it anyway.

It was a very awkward phase over the next little while as the substitute landlord wannabe tagged along behind me whenever I showed up at the fourplex. Somehow I had inherited a stray dog or something.

So, this guy successfully graduated out of the DB category into some other series that I have yet to name. I'll leave him paired up with the golf bag sandwich for now, just in case there's further mutation. So beware of Dust Bunnies. I can't make it any clearer than that.

Now don't get me wrong. I'm sure everyone has slotted me into the Landlord category, and you can imagine the baggage that goes with that. Well, I'm doing it to them, so fair is fair.

Oh, and I hesitate to mention the Lay Away category. I hesitate a lot.

Chapter 71

Philosophies

It was simple. A philosophy a day kept insanity away. Philosophies were the lifelines to reality, drawing me out from the depths of despair. I just called them Fills, which was short for the "phil" in philosophy. Fills did what they were supposed to do, and that was to fill in the gaps between sanities so I could always make it back to the right one. My favorite one for a long time was: "Don't worry, tomorrow is another day." The only problem with that one was I was using it every day. That became very depressing, so I moved to another Fill: "Plan or die." It only lasted a couple of days. What was I thinking?

One Fill came naturally. A tenant phoned and said the water tank had "exploded." I ran to the car, taking a shortcut so that I could bang my head on a branch hanging down from a tree. While still half in a daze and bleeding, I found out the real message that was supposed to have been passed to me was that the water tank was "overloaded" and not "exploded," and there was no hot water from too many people taking showers. My Fill from then on was: "Jumping to conclusions brings on contusions."

"A stitch in time saves nine" only lasted a little while, too. There were too many giant rips in my life to mend before I could care about a stupid stitch being out of whack.

"What goes around comes around" was my best soother. With that Fill I always had the pleasure of imagining a certain situation falling in someone else's lap. I didn't want them to burn at the stake or anything, but I liked to think that it didn't all just happen to me. The simplest fantasy was hoping they would all be Landlords some day.

One Fill I found I was using a lot was: "What's that got to do with the price of bread?" I found this one brought everything down to a common denominator and put things into perspective. "Bread" was the topic. Stick to it, and stop telling me about your Aunt Agnes in Texas so we can concentrate on getting your rent.

"Time heals all wounds" was my long-term soother. It ranked right up there with that silver lining thing with the clouds. But it started to feel like an escape from reality. The reality was: I got wounded, and even though I knew I would heal someday, whose life did I have the privilege of making miserable while I healed?

Banks had their own Fills: "We're stopping payment on your reality cheque." You see, there are only two job classifications at a bank. Either you're a Manager or you're an Assistant Manager. It doesn't matter if it's your first day on the job at the bank, you'll fit into one of these job titles. So, since you can't be absolutely sure that they're giving you the straight goods in their answers, it brought up the one and only response that got their attention and brought solutions. Quite simply, I said, "I bet another bank would like to carry my mortgages." You wouldn't believe how many fees and charges have been waived since I got that new line. I figure since it's illegal to kill them, I might as well fall back on something.

Looking at the big picture, you have to realize that Earth is just one big insane asylum in our solar system. That's why, if you complain too much, God will make you live longer. So this brings in my paranoid Fill: "The situation is hopeless and yes, they are out to get you." I only use this when I feel very low on the food chain.

The ultimate Fill that works on just about everything is: "I really don't care, and I don't have to." This takes care of all the stupid things that happen to me that would normally be funny if they weren't happening to me all the time. If I find myself screwing up something that was guaranteed to be idiot-proof, I have to reach for my "It's OK" Fill. Actually, it's not OK, but at least I have the safe feeling that I'm not working with subatomic particles where something could blow up.

Last, but not least, is a simple Fill: "Not today." Some days I think that if I were to take an IQ test I wouldn't get any points at all. "Not today" saves a lot of embarrassment and makes me look busy at the same time. Plus, it's only two words and not too hard to remember.

But having Fills isn't enough. I always figured I had some sort of Guardian Angel looking out for me. I had to, because I couldn't possibly explain how I've made it this far in one piece. Take yesterday, for example. I was in one of the suites replacing a light fixture that wasn't working. I told the tenant to turn off the electrical circuit in the breaker box. "Sure," he said, and off he went. He was back in a flash and I was just about ready to expose the wiring when I thought, "Why am I assuming that this guy understands the difference between a fuse box and a watermelon?"

So I got down from the stepladder and sure enough, the power was on. Oh, the fridge was shut down just beautifully in case I was going to work on it next, but the light was all powered up just waiting to fry me up for dinner. That was one I chalked up to the Angel watching me.

Not five minutes later as I was leaving, I just got to my car parked in the driveway when I realized I had left the old light fixture back in the suite. Might be fixable, I thought. Went back in and ten seconds later, BANG. One of the other tenants had come screaming into the driveway so fast with his car he took out the back end of mine. I figured if I had been sitting in the car, I'd have a neck that was five inches longer, with whiplash all the way down to my toenails. He wanted to know if his rental damage deposit would cover it. Thanks again, Angel, for getting me out of that one, but if you are at all responsible for sending me that idiot in the first place, well, stop it, okay?

Phone Message Light Flashing

- It's Bob calling back. There's a small glitch with the electrical connection on the water tank, Fred. You'll need to call an electrician in to get it hooked up and running.

- Me again. Remember when the water tank overflowed on to the carpet? It's starting to smell funny.

- This is the Appliance Center getting back to you. I checked out your oven at 607 and all you needed was a new fuse to get it going. I'm afraid the minimum charge for a house call is $50.00. Plus parts, of course. Thanks.

- This is the Accounts Administrator from the Bank calling back. We did that name check you requested and we do not have a client by that name.

- Fred, this is your Insurance Company calling back. Sorry, bud, you're not covered for that item we discussed.

Chapter 72

Reward System vs. Bonus System

Sometimes life is one great big bowl of cherries. I usually come to that conclusion when I'm finishing up my six-pack. The rest of the time it comes down to prioritizing the good times around the more unpleasant tasks in my life. That brings the Reward System into play. Everyone does it; it's just a matter of how we all carry it out. For instance, if I collect all the rent on the first of the month, I take the whole family out to dinner. That, unfortunately, has never happened.

If I reconcile my bank statements with Bev's withdrawals, I treat myself to lunch at the local pub. I still don't know what kind of draft beer they have on tap.

If I could just get by only one month without a flippin' appliance breaking down, I don't know what I'd do, because that will never happen.

So you can see my Reward System doesn't pay off too well, so that's why I moved over to my Bonus System. It's more flexible. For instance, if I didn't hurt myself putting a new washer in a sink, bonus. Didn't run over the petunias with the lawn mower, bonus. Remembered to turn the sprinklers off before going to bed, bonus.

As you can see, this system is more of a don't-wreck-anything scenario, compared to the rigid Reward System. The bonuses are cooling off in the fridge.

Chapter 73

Intensity

Intensity. Any day you can expect a hot iron rod to pierce your heart. Are you up for the challenge, or are you going to let it slip through your chest like warm butter? They're trying to skewer you, you shishkabob!

That's my recorded message on my alarm clock. I hear that every day. I need a boost to get me going in the morning. It's the difference between drinking a cup of coffee in the morning and splashing the coffee straight onto your face. Sometimes it's a combo. I sit there drinking it at the table, then doze off until my nose lands in the cup and gets burnt.

Sometimes I'll have a Slurpee in the afternoon. I know it gives me brain freeze, but it's the closest I'll ever get to empathizing with my tenants. I don't mean to be intense, I just got that way somehow. It's a little like the "dog-eat-dog" Fill that people use, but I like to think of it more like completing my tasks using creative chaos. You see, "normal" just doesn't feed the bulldog anymore (another Fill).

Creative chaos is both a personal challenge and a public concern. Like the time one of my tenants gave me a cheque for the rent after his last one bounced. This time when I went to the bank, I presented the cheque and asked if the funds were available. Naturally, I was right and the bank said no. The key here is that I still had the cheque with me with no bank stamp showing insufficient funds on it. Sure enough, the tenant used every excuse in his handbook, and then just took off in the middle of the night partway through the month. I just patiently kept going to his bank over the next six weeks until, lo and behold, one day he had the available funds. So I cashed the cheque.

Thank you, Mr. Tenant. If you need a reference, don't hesitate to ask.

Phone Message Light Flashing

- This is the electrician calling back. It's worse then I thought so you had better call me before I do anything else.

- Fred, I presume I'm getting a break in this month's rent with me having no hot water and all. I figure half a month is fair.

- This is the Better Business Bureau returning your call. Could you please come in to pick up the information concerning that plumber you hired. There's way too many pages to fax. Thanks.

- The reason your furnace isn't working is because you're out of fuel. I'll have to make another trip to re-boot it after you get some oil delivered. I'm afraid I have to charge you for two house calls.

- Me again, sorry, bud, you're not covered for that either.

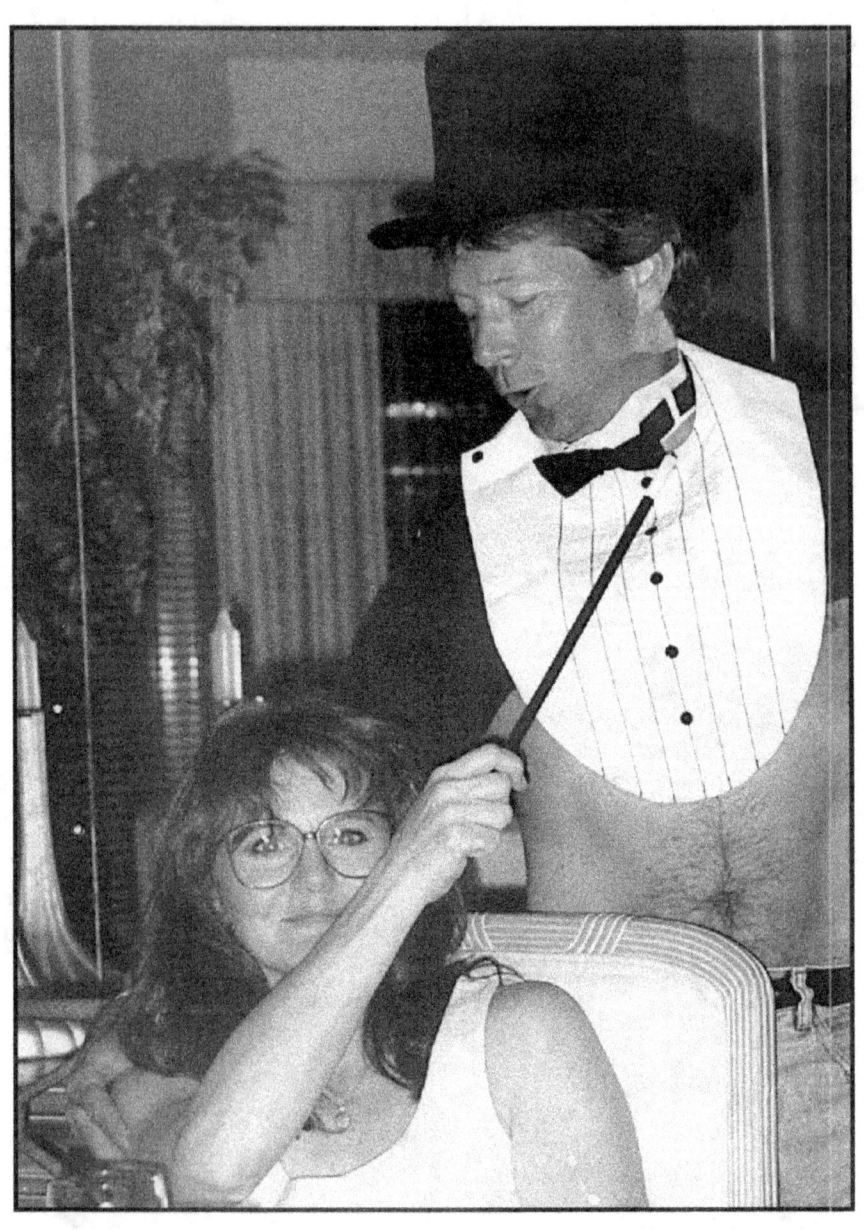

Bev & Fred

Chapter 74

The Magic of Cooking

One day Bev showed me where the stove was. She said, "Cook."

I only knew how to cook two things. I knew how to order out any kind of food she wanted, but that wasn't frying. I had to progress beyond steak and corn. I started with cookbooks, but I never seemed to have all the ingredients. By the time I got through reading my twentieth recipe I still didn't have a dish to make. But, by then, I had cooking all figured out. The recipes I had read were pretty much the same. They just had different ingredients. So I thought I might as well use what we had, and create my own dishes.

The first dish was Revenue Canada Stew. I called it that because by the time I finished making it, I had pretty well cleaned out the whole fridge. I'd give you the recipe, but the instructions are so complicated you wouldn't understand them. Bev says I make it far too hot and spicy, and that it "burns going down." I told her that was the whole point of Revenue Canada Stew. By the way, this is the most expensive dish to make.

Another dish I enjoyed making was Tenant Turnovers. Naturally, it's a simple dish. I just use some puff pastry and stuff it with a little hamburger, bologna and sausage. The key here is to keep it inexpensive so that if you don't like them, you won't mind throwing them out.

Banker's Pasta is another one of my favorites. First, you cook the pasta until it's all fat and puffy. You will notice that pastas all look and taste exactly the same. The key here is to give it some color and taste, because pasta by itself is incredibly boring. The great thing is that just about any sauce you put on Banker's Pasta will improve it. Actually, the more you can cover up the pasta with spices, the better.

Another dish made to be grilled on the BBQ is City Hall Sizzlers. This dish is meant to be cooked very, very slowly. The Sizzler dish requires you to skewer anything you can get hold of and grill it. Always make sure none of the skewers are the same, and don't be afraid to make as many as you want.

One of the handiest dishes is Landlord Soup. This dish can be prepared ahead of time and left in the fridge, in the dark, for days. One of the key features of this soup is that it seems to be okay if it boils over. The main difference between RC Stew and this dish is that RC Stew is thick, and LS is runny. Also, it's impossible to make LS after you have made RC Stew because there are no ingredients left. Be cautious about other people helping you make this soup. A lot of people want to add bull meat. Even though LS does not need any bull, somehow it always ends up with some. Onions are a key ingredient to the overall success of this soup. Always place your face directly over the onions while cutting them. Lastly, a rich red wine is recommended with this dish. Usually two to three quarts will do the trick.

This last dish is a classic: Stuffed Real E-Steak in a Rich and Heavy Cream Sauce. You can tell by the name that it's really big and, trust me, you can get it anywhere. It's so popular that some people will actually send you brochures outlining their recipes, and some will even be so bold as to knock on your door trying to sell their dish. Unfortunately, it's very expensive to make. It's one of those dishes where the family better get together before deciding to make this particular baby.

Simply, the steak is filleted down the middle and stuffed with expensive seafood that you can't see. Everyone seems to think they have the best secret way to cook it but, in the end, they usually all get the same result. You can broil, BBQ, panfry, grill, microwave or bake it. You can do almost anything you want, but DO NOT steam it. Steaming is left for all the other things you have to do after you've decided to make Real E-Steak. The key here is to marinate the E-Steak before cooking. And, believe it or not, E-Steak can soak and wallow in a beer marinade for days! That's right; I bet you didn't know that.

As far as the sauce goes, let your imagination run rampant. You've already spent a lot of money, so don't be afraid to go for the gusto. You can substitute gravy for the sauce if you want. But don't forget, if someone says, "Your gravy is lumpy," you tell them, "Those are teeny-weeny dumplings you're experiencing, and they took a long time to make!"

This dish goes great with Banker's Pasta for some reason. The three quarts of wine recommended as an accompaniment for Landlord Soup should be doubled when serving this dish.

So, as you see, cooking mimics life. Enjoy!

Chapter 75

Send in the Substitute Landlord

I was leafing through Bev's lettuce in the fridge one day looking for hidden beers when I got this idea. Why shouldn't I hide, just like my beer, and hire someone else to be the Landlord and take care of the suites? I knew this was a good idea because the beer began to taste extra smooth, plus I found a bonus beer under the cobs of corn to confirm the good idea.

I phoned some rental agencies and basically found out that it was going to cost me a lot of money for them to rent out the suites plus collect the rent. As far as repairs went, that was still going to be my headache. So I ditched that idea and, all of a sudden, the second beer didn't taste as good as the first one.

That's when Bev walked by. Bad timing for her, because now I had another idea and the beer was back to tasting good again.

It was Bev's turn to fly with the tenants. My job was starting to take me out of town anyway and, other than taking care of Sammy, Bev wasn't working. Actually, Bev wasn't my first choice. If Godzilla had been available I would have hired him. Anyway, although I had all the confidence in the world with my Bevy, I was really only hoping to squeeze a year out of her as the new Landlord. I figured the break would rejuvenate me long enough to get back into the ring for a couple more rounds.

I quickly learned when it was time to hide in the garage and avoid her. The most obvious one, of course, was when she went out to collect rent. On those occasions, I spent the maximum allowable time (two hours) hiding. If it was a phone call from a tenant, then I would slip outside for fifteen minutes. When I saw a bounced cheque in the mail, I would stay at least fifteen feet from the letter. As Bev got closer to the letter, I got closer to the back door. I only had to stay in the garage until the car door slammed and I heard her speed away.

Bev had never said a bad four-letter word in her life. In her new role as substitute Landlord, though, she soon adopted expletives as common adjectives for everyday things. Even my fried egg in the morning was being verbally abused. I figured it was time to step in and take over, because I really didn't like seeing her destroy herself. Besides, I was really getting tired of spending so much time in the garage. But she was a true champ. She said she would continue taking care of the suites, even if it killed her. I told her that it looked like she only had a couple more weeks to live, and I'd miss her when she was gone.

This one time (and don't you ever tell Bev I told you this!), she got a cheque sent back from the bank NSF for the third time in the same month, from the same tenant. I'm not kidding you, her muscles doubled in size, she picked up the receipt book like it was a bazooka, and got in the car like it was an armored tank. I was married to Rambo. Sammy and I set up camp in the garage and observed a moment of silence for the tenant.

To this day, I don't know what happened to the guy. I kept reading the front page of the newspaper to see if there were any related headlines that would give me a clue to his whereabouts, plus I kept an eye on the obituaries for his name. All I know is that Bev had this Mona Lisa smile for a few days, and I just had to assume that she had taken care of the matter to her own satisfaction. I'd bet you that poor sucker is still digging himself out of the hole Bev buried him in.

Banks took on a whole new meaning now that she had rent money to deposit. Bev's only previous experience had been taking money out of a bank. Reversing the process was a new concept for her, and it was kind of fun to watch.

Don't forget, she had three mortgage payments she had to make. (Well, more like tried to make.) Anyway, she sure met a lot of new people at the bank.

One benefit was that Sam and I got to go out and hit a bucket of golf balls at the driving range once a month. That's when the bank statements arrived in the mail. We didn't want Sam to pick up any bad words when Mommy was balancing the chequing account. Bev lasted the year. Her learning curve was huge. She didn't gain any respect for me having done it for the past nine years, because it was offset by me being stupid enough to get us into it in the first place. But we came to the common ground that I was hoping for from the beginning. We shared the headache.

I immediately took her to Las Vegas as a well-deserved reward.

Chapter 76

Another Day, Another Life

So the days went by, and I was reminded of the Fill, "If you always do what you've always done, you'll always get what you've always gotten." I guess that's why the days went by.

I had an argument with one of my tenants. He was this big, burly tow truck driver. I don't know what I was doing arguing with him in the first place. I couldn't take this guy down with a rocket launcher. I got my car towed one day for parking illegally, by a different tow truck driver, and had an argument with him. I finally realized that this was normal for tow truck drivers, so I avoided future arguments with my tenant until one day when he decided to tow one of my other tenants' cars away because they parked in his spot. I ended up solving the problem by phoning the police and telling them that the car was stolen. I didn't answer my door for the next few days. I made some Tenant Turnovers to cheer me up.

On top of all this, I work for a living. Yup, get up in the morning, burn my toast, feed the cat, and forget to turn off the coffee pot on my way out the door. When I finally leave work at the end of the day, I just go to my next job as the Landlord. I call it Fred's Emporium now, because anything goes at anytime, rain or shine.

I had to go to the suites one day to fix something. I parked under the carport and noticed some nice potted plants on the balcony above. Wow, I thought. Someone is actually trying to make the place look good. When I finished fixing the problem, I couldn't help but notice that one of the potted plants had fallen off the balcony and landed smack dab in the middle of my car hood. I went home and threw out the Tenant Turnovers.

So I'm blessed with five senses, okay? Not really. My sense of feeling is very numb. I really don't **feel** well. Sight? You wouldn't believe what I saw in one of the suites today. I don't consciously wish to be blind or anything, but I really didn't want to see that. My hearing is fine. I hear natter-natter all flippin' day long just fine. If, for some reason, they don't think I heard their natter-natter, they'll be sure to repeat it. Sense of smell? Don't really care. Doesn't do anything for me, as opposed to my sense of taste. The first beer tastes as good as the last beer. Thank God one of my senses makes sense.

One other thing that rattles all my senses is HYDRO BILLS! Hydro bills get me down. The two illegal suites in the fourplex have to pay a percentage of the hydro bill from the top suites. It's a 33-67 split, based on the suites upstairs being bigger, usually with more people in them. When the bill comes in, neither side hesitates to call me and say:

"They keep their windows open with the heat on. I'm not paying."

"They do laundry all day long, and I just do it once a week."

"They leave their lights on, so why should I pay for that?"

"They're always taking a shower, and their friends use the showers too."

"I think they should pay more." (Bottom suites.)

"I think they should pay more." (Top suites.)

Like, what am I supposed to do? Confiscate all the light bulbs and shut down the hot water tank? One day the hydro did get cut off on one side. Lots of fun sorting that one out, because we're talking bounced cheques from tenants who had already left with their security deposits. I hate hydro bills.

So, finally, I get a phone call that's not a tenant complaining about the hydro bill. It's a collection agency. They tell me that I am now responsible for payments to the tune of $220 for a flute that I had co-signed for. The owner has skipped town and I am now legally responsible for the payments.

Simple questions come to mind. "What flute are you talking about, and where's the hidden camera?" Because I must be on some sort of TV show, and I'm being filmed with the hopes that I'm going to act real funny in front of the audience and maybe win the $10,000 grand prize.

Ends up that one of my tenants forged my signature on the purchase of a flute, and I was now the proud owner of the rest of the payments. I wouldn't pay, and for that I got to be harassed and registered with all sorts of Better Business Bureau type companies as a "DON'T DO BUSINESS WITH THIS CROOK BECAUSE HE'LL STEAL EVERYTHING YOU HAVE!" credit risk.

Anyway, it's just another day, and it's bound to get better.

Chapter 77

It's Raining

I was at work and I got a call from one of my neighbors. He said it was raining in one of my suites. I told him that was impossible because the weather guy in the paper had predicted clear skies. He said he was sorry to give me the bad news, but it was raining in my suite nonetheless. I asked him if he had any other good news for me, and he said, "No, but have a nice day."

I went to my boss to tell him I had to go because it was raining in my suite. He asked, "Cumulus or nimbus?" I said I would find out. He said he was sorry to hear the bad news, but I assured him it was okay. At least there hadn't been any lightning strikes reported.

I had to drive home to get the keys to the suite. The tenants were out when I arrived there around 11:30. Sure enough, there was rain coming down from the ceiling in the living room, kitchen and pantry. It was about a half-inch deep in some places. I thought, you can't get them to water the flippin' grass, but they somehow have the time to water the suite.

I went upstairs to see what was going on. There it was: the water in the kitchen sink was turned on full with the stopper in. The place was flooded. I should have brought my fishing rod. When I turned off the water and drained the sink, I noticed that he had two glasses and a plate in the sink. Yeah, I thought. It takes 5,000 gallons of water to wash two glasses and a plate. Later, I found out that he had left for work at 8:00 that morning. I wondered how many gallons could come out of a tap in three-and-a-half hours.

I got the insurance guy to come over. He couldn't believe the mess. He asked if the tenant had insurance so he could pay for it. I told him to look around at the tenant's furniture and then ask the same question again. "No need," he said.

They had to replace the carpet in both living rooms and the linoleum in both kitchens, as well as put in a new ceiling. Most of the walls had to be ripped out and replaced. It took five weeks of construction, and I'm happy to say I didn't have to do anything but pick out the colors.

In the end, the tenant said he was sorry and wouldn't do it again. I looked around at all the new carpets and flooring, and asked him if he would consider moving to the fourplex. Lots of room for improvement over there, I thought.

Doing dumb things isn't limited to just the tenants. By the time Friday rolls around I'm usually down to my last brain cell from working all week. The remaining brain cell is all I've got left to use on the weekend to do all the Landlording stuff. Thank goodness it mutates, so that I've got something to start with on Monday morning. Either that, or somehow I suck up the tenants' brain cells. Scary thought, but that could explain a lot of things.

For instance, the other day I went to spray one of my bushes because there were bugs on it. Good idea, except I used the wrong bottle and sprayed it with a non-selective herbicide that kills everything except Morning Glory. The bush was dead within a week. There weren't any bugs on it anymore, so technically I had accomplished my task. When I had to explain it to Bev, I blamed the death of the bush on the dog: "His favorite potty spot," as I pointed to the dead bush.

There were other things that I did with mind-numbing accuracy. Like driving all the way over to the fourplex just so I could forget why I drove over there. Oh sure, I'll remember when Bev asks me, "Did you get it?" and I'll say, "The tenant wasn't home." Then the phone will ring and it's the tenant wondering where I am, because she's still waiting for me.

The shortage of brain cells causes other problems as well. Like standing in a grocery store without a clue why you're there. I can't believe how many times I've had to share my steak with the cat because I forgot to get cat food. I always seem to be one slice short of a regular pepperoni pizza.

The brain cells just don't multiply fast enough.

Phone Message Light Flashing

- One of your tenants called me because the power went out in her suite. It was just the breaker switch that had tripped. I'm afraid I'll have to charge you for the service call. I'll send you an invoice in the mail.

- Fred, this is your dentist's office calling. You missed your appointment today. We do have to charge if you don't give us 24 hours notice. How's next Tuesday for you? We should allow at least two hours to do your root canal.

- Mr. Miller, I'm afraid your stove is totally shot. About the only thing working is that new fuse I put in last week.

- This is the Tenancy Branch calling again. This is the third time you have missed an arbitration meeting. You will have to pay the $35.00 processing fee for all three meetings. A new arbitration date will be sent to you in the mail.

Chapter 78

Reference Checks

I always enjoy giving reference checks for my tenants to other prospective Landlords. I especially like the ones where the tenant hasn't told me he's leaving yet. That usually makes for a very short reference check. Sometimes, prospective Landlords don't ask the right questions. Like, "Do they pay their rent by cheque or cash?"

I tell them cheque. What they should have asked me was, "Do the cheques bounce?" Now we're getting somewhere.

They ask me something like, "Are they pleasant people to rent to?" Who cares? I'd rather rent to unpleasant people who pay the rent and keep the place clean than to pleasant people who don't.

I don't do reference letters. One time this tenant offered to draft me a reference letter for my signature. "Go for it," I told her. Next thing I know she presents me with this three-page letter with her work resume attached. The resume was so thick that I figured the only thing missing was her being Queen of the Nile for a two-week term. I signed it. I figured anyone gullible enough to believe this thing needs a life lesson. I always get a kick out of the ones who "moved here from back East" and therefore don't have references. I get their name and number, and look it up in the telephone book. Eighty percent of the time it's there. One hundred percent of the time I don't rent to them.

There's only one way to find out if the person standing in front of you is going to pay the rent and be a good tenant. Unfortunately, it took me ten years to figure it out. You see, it's not by the car they drive or the clothes they wear. Anybody can fake you out with that. Charm and charisma are other forms of disguising a less than desirable tenant. No, there's just one way.

You tell them that, as their new Landlord, you will be seeing them at the beginning of each month to collect rent. If you can't find them, they are supposed to find you. Then you tell them that from the second of the month until the end of the month, you do not collect rent. You tell them that's what Bubba is paid to do. Then you watch their face. If they have to ask who Bubba is, that's one strike. "Does Bubba have a key to the place?" is strike two. If they're already running away, that's strike three. The thing is, you don't really need a real Bubba. The imagination is a wonderful thing.

Chapter 79

Attitude

I started to realize that I had somehow copped an attitude. I blamed it on society, because everyone else blames society for everything that goes wrong. If there was an Ann Landers Attitude Test, I probably wouldn't take it, because I really don't care.

I really noticed my attitude one day when the new shed I had just built at the fourplex got broken into the day after it was finished. I just sat and stared at the broken door and the big emptiness that shouldn't have been there. All my neighbor's tools were gone. I looked around, and most of the tenants were staring out the windows. I guess my attitude was showing, because they weren't coming down to talk to me.

The insurance guy came over. He looked at me and said, "I didn't know you had another place." I said, "There's more." Ended up with $500 in new tools and equipment. Soon after that my own house was broken into. Didn't lose a lot, but the insurance guy wasn't impressed when he saw me again. The following year my insurance premiums went up and I didn't get the usual Christmas card. Just for that, I'm going to invent a casserole named after you.

Even my neighbor had an attitude. "I know you've got an illegal suite in your house, and if you don't get rid of him I'm going to phone City Hall and report you." Bad timing for him because I had an attitude too!

I figured this called for some devious tactics, so I immediately thanked him for helping Bev and me out with a very difficult decision. You could tell by the look on his face he wasn't expecting that. (I'd had this make-believe plan up my sleeve for a long time waiting for a day just like this.)

I started to walk away and sure enough he called over, "Hey Fred, exactly how did I help you and Bev out?" Well, that's when I pointed over to the side of my house. I told him about our plan to get a rezoning permit to build an addition on to the side of the house and turn it into a multi-unit complex. "You'd be surprised at how close I'm allowed to build this complex to your property line," I told him. "It's sure going to be noisy around here for a while with all that construction going on."

Well, the conversation didn't last too much longer after that. All of a sudden my illegal suite didn't seem to be that big a deal after all.

"Let sleeping dogs lie," was his last comment on the subject. I told him I would do my best to convince Bev that he didn't want us to build our dream complex. I figured this was a good time to borrow some tools from him, so I got his table saw.

I try to fix or make something right for at least someone or something every week. That was my motto for a long time. "Unfortunately," I tell them these days, "this is not your week, and it doesn't look very good for you in the future, either."

This is the heart of the attitude problem. "Where the heck did I cop an attitude like that?" I thought to myself. So it's time for an attitude adjustment. Time to spice up my life and get back to Fred's Fun Zone, which happens to be the workshop where I keep all the beer in one of my many fridges. It was time to roll up my sleeves and start a new project!

I decided to bash the kitchen wall out (which was on the second floor) and put in sliding glass doors, and then wrap a brand new sundeck around most of the house. According to my diagram, the deck would end up being 1,400 square feet in total. Even though the last deck I built was only 120 square feet, I felt that the experience I got from that deck qualified me somewhat for this new design. I could feel a real attitude adjustment when I stood back and studied my design. Maybe because all my body parts that had been injured in the past were starting to come to life again.

I was definitely smiling when I started to put the finishing touches on my sketch of the deck. I was wondering if I could build it real quick and somehow surprise Bev. I was also smiling because I didn't have an old deck to rip down like the last time. That was going to save a lot of time, plus the wear and tear on my car. And I'd get to see all my buddies at City Hall again.

Well, to make a long story short, it took three months of dealing with City Hall to get my permit, and just a bunch of weekends for me and my Dad, with a little help from my friends, to get it built. One of the neighbors asked if I was building a ferry terminal. The whole block asked to see my building permit.

Just to make the deadline to finish the deck more fun, Bev and I planned to host her parents' fiftieth wedding anniversary at our house. The last support nail went in at 4:00 and the party, complete with eighty guests, was due to kick off at 5:00. At one count, the deck was safely holding sixty-two people. I wasn't one of them.

Well, to say the least, I was proud of my deck. It was a great party, and I had a new attitude. Motto of the story: *"Feel like heck, build a deck."*

Chapter 80

Landlord School

I don't try to impress anyone. I'm just humble little me, but every so often one of my tenants asks me how they can become a Landlord. I just love that question. Usually I start off by getting information from them. It usually goes something like this:

"How many suites do you want to own?" I ask. I find this question suggests to them that they can start tomorrow with several suites if they want to.

"Six or seven to start out with." A typical response.

Then I ask them, "What rent do you want to charge?" At this point you can see their eyes light up. They can't believe they hadn't thought of doing this years before. They should be millionaires by the time the year is out.

I get answers like, "A thousand bucks a suite." Or, "It depends if they have a view of the ocean." At this point they're revved up. They're ready to have a city named after them. Now it's time to hit them with a few reality checks. I start off with the small solvable ones, then I work up to the mind-numbing questions.

"Will you allow pets?" I inquire, as if this is going to make or break the whole thing.

"Sure," they say. "No problem." That's when I shake my head ever so slightly and sigh. I tell them a couple of stories, and within minutes they've changed their mind to **No Pets Allowed!**

I always inquire about yard maintenance. "Who's going to do that?" I ask. At this point they become a little confused and disoriented. They know as a tenant they don't do it. None of the other tenants do it. So, as a Landlord, they'll have to do it. The eyes aren't quite as large anymore.

A typical response is, "My girlfriend likes gardening." If they think deeper for a minute, they sometimes realize that the girlfriend doesn't do it either. At this point you want to get them excited about it again, so you ask them if they are prepared to set up a business account to track all this new money that's going to be pouring in.

Now that their eyes are wide open again, I inform them that they will need some kind of deposit to start the ball rolling. They never seem to ask just how much that will be, but they all assure me that this isn't a problem. Yeah right, didn't your cheque bounce last month?

At this point they start fidgeting. Too many highs and lows mixed with confusion. They know there's more, but they're not sure what they want to know. That's where I step in with a little more advice.

"With your new Landlord status, you should be able to retire early." They get an instant high.

"Of course, you have to factor in vacancies and property taxes." Instant low.

"But, as you probably know, there is a lot of property maintenance involved in owning your own buildings, but that is all a tax write-off." Medium high.

"But that will affect your Capital Gains with Revenue Canada." Deep low.

I usually like to leave it there. If I keep the last two words of the conversation as "Revenue Canada," it has more of a lasting impression. Usually, at this point, the person has to leave anyway.

I feel glad that I could help them out.

Chapter 81

They're Back

Revenue Canada was back in my face again. They didn't like the losses I was declaring. Like I was supposed to tell them I made money, and excuse me for spending money on my tenants and not being a slum Landlord. Anyway, they had already taxed the money when I earned it; now they wanted to tax it again. Would you please untax me a little, thank you very much.

I met with a Revenue Canada representative. We were barely ten seconds into the interview when I realized this was an inquisition and not an interview. He looked like a cloned space alien from a nearby galaxy. No forked tongue or anything like that, but I really felt some sort of power surge from him.

Neither one of us understood how much I owed. I was told that there was no dollar limit, so don't plan on going anywhere. I told him the only way I could possibly pay more money was to use my credit line. I mentioned the $25,000 ceiling. He smiled, knowing that he finally had a target to shoot for. More Revenue Canada people were brought in. Through the whispers, I believed they were discussing the value of the shirt on my back. I hoped they would leave me something to wear on my way home.

I think I dealt with a dozen Revenue Canada representatives. Every time I wore one of them out, they sent in a fresh one. They were all graduates of the "How to Suck Every Drop of Emotion Out of Your Client" seminar. They all graduated with honors. Mentally, I was not Fred anymore. I was a dribbling, babbling mess.

I remember crawling into bed that night. I curled up in a fetal position to feel safer. I was just short of sucking my thumb. I didn't have any food in the fridge because I'd had Revenue Canada Stew the other night. I couldn't even order a pizza. Somehow Revenue Canada had garnisheed all my pizza-ordering privileges. I tried to think of a Fill to help me get back on track.

I could only come up with, "A fool and his money are soon parted."

Phone Message Light Flashing

- This is Sergeant Smith calling from the Police Station. It seems there was an incident at one of your properties today and we need you to come down and make a statement. You may want to consider having some legal representation with you.

- We'll have to come back and clean your carpet again. We can't guarantee that we'll get that stain out but we did eliminate most of the smell.

- Hey bud, your insurance policy runs out at the end of the month. Let's set up a time.

Chapter 82

Video Game

Being a Landlord is a lot like a video game. You don't get three lives, though. The object of the game is to score points that equate to dollars. The more points you get, the better you do, but you have to be careful because you can lose points just as easily.

The game runs on a monthly cycle and, at the end of every month, you move to another level. The new level is based on how well you did at the last level. Points are scored mainly at the beginning of the level, based on how well you "collect rent." In order to get your points, you have to shoot at the Tenants' Secret Handbook. It always stands in front of the rent and must be destroyed, or you get no points.

Once the handbook is destroyed, you have to catch the rent. The rent is allowed to run anywhere it wants, and you have to find it. But even when you've found it, you still don't get any points until you find the secret door to the "bank vault." The vault will let you know if the points are good or not. This particular level is not limited to the monthly cycle. It can be carried over to other cycles indefinitely.

Throughout the game you have to watch out for the "Point Robbers." These robbers do not have to play the game by the rules and, as they grow, they invent new rules. The object of the game is to either destroy them or run far away from them. The "Arbitrator Traitors" can only be released by the tenants. Once released, they are unavoidable, and you must give them back valuable points. They have a tendency to mutate if not confronted.

The "Revenue Rovers" are very powerful. They give you rules

on how to play the game, but they do not have to follow the rules themselves. These Rovers are allowed to stop the game at any point and penalize you for points. The penalties are random and cannot be revoked. The game does not have any weapons to stop the Rovers.

Throughout the game, the Landlord must "perform maintenance" in order for the game to continue. The object is to pick up the little symbols that appear as you wander through the game. Common symbols are hammers, sinks, stoves and pipes. You have to give back points to pick up these items, but you may find yourself in a particular segment of the game where, if you have one of these symbols, you save points. These symbols must be given each year to the Revenue Rovers, who store them and bring them out every seven years for review.

The "City Hallers" are hard to spot. They are buried under paper and only come alive when you step on one. If confronted by a Haller, it is best to run. Hallers don't necessarily cost you points, but they keep you from getting points by making you stop. It's very much like the Go Directly to Jail square in Monopoly.

To keep the game interesting, it introduces random "Irritants." These are allowed to roam anywhere throughout the game, and range from mild to extreme. They have been known to take points, but their main purpose is to lower the energy level of the Landlord and replace it with stress. The Irritants only stop if the Landlord calls an official time-out by checking into a hospital.

The whole game is controlled by the Money Bags. This group owns the Bank Vault, and the only reason you're allowed to play this game is because these Baggers let you. The good news is, the Baggers act like they are on your side because they want you to get all those valuable points. The bad news is that they want you to give all the points back to them after you do all the collecting. These Baggers have the ability to blow the entire game up if you don't play by their rules. The only way to get rid of the Baggers is to pay back all the points you owe them. (Plus all the handling fees they make up.) When that finally happens, you die of old age the following week. The Baggers often like to refer to this dying process as "amortization."

So far, you might be wondering why you should play this game. It doesn't sound like much fun. Well, let's introduce the "Idiots." This group can be annoying and, yes, cost you time and effort, but they can be a lot of fun. Idiots are found throughout the game and they can easily be disabled and picked apart once you learn how to use your "sarcastic blaster." This weapon is not easy to use. It must hit the tiny brain of the Idiot, sometimes several times, before it works.

One of the other great features of the Idiot group is that all the other players in the game are allowed to gang up on the Idiots. It's the only time that all players put forth a team effort. Sometimes you think you've dismantled all of them and the next thing you know, they're all back again. They're everywhere, but they truly are a lot of fun to have around.

Another important feature of the game is "Family." Family influences the Landlord in different directions, and can be very helpful if you find yourself stuck somewhere in the game. Family will also give you directions, even when you don't ask for them. But here's where the bonus points come in. They offer free meals and refreshments if you listen to their advice. This sometimes sways the Landlord's decision-making process, but hey, that's just the way the game is.

One day the Landlord will finally get tired of the game and want to quit. This introduces the last figure in the game called the "Get Real Estater." This character is a point killer. Throughout the whole game you see them, but you're allowed to close the door on them so they don't bother you. But if you keep the door open too long, they all want to come in. In the end, the Get Real Estater is the only one who can unplug the game and let you go home, so you pretty much have to deal with one of them sometime.

One of the unfortunate aspects of the game is that if you play too long, the Revenue Rovers don't want to stop playing. Even if you say, "I'm finished," they will still continue to play with you for up to seven years. They will actually continue to change the rules and then go back to the symbols you gave them and look for more points. The more points they find, the hungrier they get. And when one of them finds these points, they tell other Rovers, who join in on the feast.

When it's finally over, most people destroy the game or try to pass it on to some tenants they know.

Chapter 83

Fetch, Good Boy!

I wish someone had taught me how to roll over and play dead. Dogs learn to do it, and they get treats for doing it. "Good boy," they hear, and then they're given yum-yums. Why can't a Landlord get away with doing that?

I'll tell you what I get to do all day long. It's more like fetching sticks, that's what. I know where every hardware store is in town, and I know each of their employees personally. I make so many trips to the dump they've named a corner after me. City Hall is considering giving me my own parking spot right beside the Mayor's. My bank is considering dedicating a new wing to me with an elaborate ribbon-cutting ceremony. Why not? With the interest I've paid on my mortgages, I've more or less paid for it already.

I seem to have spent the better part of my life driving my car fetching things. No item is too small and no distance too great for Fred to go play fetch. There's always lots of time to fetch the wrong things, too. There's no reason why I can't go back and forth between stores until I finally get the item that fits. I especially like it when I can go all the way back across town to find that a seven-cent copper fitting is still on back order.

I also like to fetch big things in trucks, like dirt and sand for the garden. Bev always wants more dirt and sand so she can landscape. I guess her definition of landscaping is keeping all the sand in a big pile at the end of the driveway so Hormone can have the ultimate kitty litter box. After doing the big dirt fetch, I get to the "'big lug." The furthest point in the yard from where the dirt sits would be where I have to lug it to. The best way to lug is to wait until it rains for a couple of days and the dirt becomes completely saturated to its maximum physical weight. If you do it just right, you can attempt to throw a shovelful of dirt without any of the dirt leaving the shovel. This maneuver is particularly good for the back. I also like to lug bark mulch. To keep the experience exciting, I only do it when the mulch is very, very dry and it is a very, very windy day. That way I get to pick splinters out of my face for days.

    Some fetching is okay. Like when I get to go out and pick up steak and beer.

Chapter 84

Tenant Conversations

Conversation #1
Morning breaks and so does another appliance. This time it was a stove. "Check your timer," I said on the phone. "If it's in the ON position, it will override your putting on the oven manually."

"But I have a turkey I have to cook for my parents."

"Check the timer," I said. "I'll walk you through the process."

"They'll be here in an hour and I have to cook the turkey and the oven doesn't work."

"Put the turkey on the phone," I said.

Conversation #2
"But why can't I apply the damage deposit to the rent for this month? It's my money."

"No, the damage deposit does not count as half a month's rent. It's for security purposes."

"I promise I'm not going to damage anything."

"I'm sure you won't, but the security deposit stays where it is."

"Well, I guess I'll have to owe you the rest of the rent."

Conversation #3
"Why are you withholding ten dollars of my damage deposit?"

"Because you left a whole bunch of rotten stuff in the fridge and I had to clean it out."

"That stuff was from the tenant who lived there before I moved in."

"You mean to tell me you worked your food items around all that stuff for eight months?"

"Yeah, I didn't know if they were coming back to get it. It's not mine."

Conversation #4
"The mirror was broken before I got here."

"We inspected the place together. Here, on this checklist under bathroom, it shows no problem."

"That's because there's no specific category on the form for mirrors. That's why we didn't put it down."

"It has a section for 'other comments.' We would have noted it there."

"I know," she said. "I thought it meant it wanted comments 'other' than the mirror."

Conversation #5
"Why are there holes in the ceiling?"

"Oh, that's just from little Johnny playing with his toy missile launcher."

"Apparently it's not just a toy. It's causing substantial damage to my ceiling."

"Don't worry, we'll fix it."

"I had to show you how to change a light bulb in your refrigerator. Now you're telling me you're going to retexture a ceiling with stucco?"

"Sure," she said. "And little Johnny will help me too, won't you, little Johnny?"

Conversation #6
"Not only did your cheque bounce, but your bank has never even heard of you."

"Oh, right. I forgot I moved all my securities to another financial institution. I wanted to diversify, but still keep my stock options open."

"You just learned these new words, didn't you?"

"Oh no, I've been trading on the open market for years, now that interest rates have dipped during the second quarter."

"I'm not going to see any rent today, am I?"

"Well, if my mutual funds fluctuate with my international equities, I should be able to balance my portfolio effectively enough to meet my obligations."

"You should run for office. You would make a fine politician."

Conversation #7

"Okay, now you know that it was wrong to try to sell my dining room light."

"Yeah, I guess I figured that since it was broken anyway, you wouldn't want it, so I thought I'd do you a favor and get rid of it for you."

"But you agree that, as the Landlord, I have to make that decision?"

"Yeah, it was lucky you got the light back before my buddy got here to buy it."

"Yeah, and it was lucky I fixed it by replacing the light bulb."

Conversation #8

"Why is there spaghetti sauce all over the walls?"

"I guess we had a little accident."

"Were you intending to clean off the little accident in the near future?"

"Oh yes, we always clean up right after any little accidents happen."

"Then how do you explain the green fuzzy stuff that looks like mold growing on your little accident?"

"Oh, I think that's the basil in the sauce you're seeing."

Conversation #9

"So we agree that little Johnny will not flush any more toys down the toilet?"

"Oh, he was just playing Aqua Man and the Secret Cave."

"Yes, but if I have to unplug your toilet one more time, I'm going to charge you money for it."

"Well, really it's your fault. You're the one who won't let him play with the rocket launcher anymore."

Conversation #10

"So you called me over here because you wanted to talk. But actually you really just want to complain. So let me get this straight. When you said you weren't upset, you actually were upset? And when you said you needed new curtains, you actually thought that I was also going to get new carpeting, appliances and wallpaper? And when you asked me to drill a new hole for the picture over here, you really meant over there?

"And you want me to listen better so that this doesn't happen again?"

Chapter 85

What I'm Really Thinking

Showing suites that are for rent is really boring. I have answered the same questions a thousand times. It's not the tenant's fault, but I've done it so many times I can, and usually do, perform it in my sleep. So, to spice it up, I sometimes say the answer they want to hear, but I think a different answer in my head.

"Oh, I'm very glad to meet you. Did you have any trouble finding the place?" *You're the fourth person I've shown this suite to today, so I'm bored out of my mind and I'm sending it to Hawaii while I wait around for you to make up your mind. Then we'll do a Vulcan Mind Meld if you want to rent the place.*

"You will notice I've completely redone all the cabinets and stained them a light brown." *Just so you can bang the heck out of them and I have to redo them when you leave.*

"Over here you'll notice that the dining room and living room have been painted." *As if it's going to highlight that junk of yours you call furniture.*

"Oh yes, I believe in an open and honest Landlord and Tenant relationship." *OK, who's going to get caught in a lie first? Maybe you should know* **I DON'T DO THE TENANCY BRANCH ANYMORE, I USE RIP, AND BUBBA HELPS ME!**

"The rent is due and payable at the beginning of the month." *Like I'm assuming you know how to read a calendar and write a cheque on an account that will cover it.*

"And over here I've installed a brand-new shower stall." *I need bacon bits for my potatoes tonight, and try not to leave the door open when you're taking a shower.*

"Well, you think about it and get back to me." *Bev wants me to pick up some coffee, too, and don't complain to me if I rent it out to someone else while I'm waiting for you to get your act together. What's your name again, anyway? Bacon bits?*

They rented the suite and stayed for a year and a half. They were great people. I was sorry to see them go.

Phone Message Light Flashing

- Mr. Miller, it's the Tenancy Branch calling. In your continued absence we have decided to rule in favor of the tenant. A copy of our decision will be sent out to you in the mail along with an invoice for $140.00 for fees incurred.

- Fred, check your mailbox. I dropped off my invoice for fixing the hot water tank and the toilet. I'll drop by later to collect. I prefer payment in cash cause the banks are closed and me and the Mrs. are off for a little vacation. The total amount owing is on page three.

- Fred, I'm not paying the rent for this month cause of the stinky carpet and all the problems you caused with the toilet and the hot water stuff. I dropped by the Tenancy Branch to see what they had to say and boy did they roll their eyes when they heard your name. Bye for now. Talk to you next month.

Chapter 86

Tenant Teasing

This is a very awkward subject for me to talk about. I know they abolished Tenant Teasing a long time ago, but I swear it happened so innocently. I was with one of my buddies on the weekend and he said, "Just for fun, mention to one of your tenants that you're thinking of putting a hot tub in the backyard. You know, the one that seats about twelve people, complete with a floating bar."

So I thought, what the heck, I'll do it just once; I can handle it. But the problem was it felt so good. Then it started to be a weekend thing and, before I realized what was happening, I found myself doing it all the time. I hid it from Bev and Sam, and I wouldn't admit that I had a problem. But one day it became too much. I finally had to come to the realization that I was hooked on this kind of stuff and I needed professional help. I was saying things like, "Do you think we can fit a pool in the backyard?" and, "Wouldn't a large stone BBQ complete with dual propane tanks look good over there?"

Tenant Teasing was controlling my life. I'd do just about anything to score my next tease. I was addicted!

I heard about Tenant Teasers Anonymous and decided to join. I had a lot of support from my family and friends, and I'm feeling much better now. I take it one day at a time. Like I said, it's a very awkward subject to talk about, but I believe that society has to realize this kind of addiction can happen to anyone, and that people shouldn't go around pretending it doesn't exist just because it doesn't happen to them. TT is a sickness, and it can be treated!

Later, I thought I might start off by blaming the problem on my childhood upbringing but, unfortunately, I had a great childhood. So I figured it must have been my school teachers who failed to properly guide me to a higher level of smartness, but I recall I was more of a problem in school than they were. So it had to be my brothers and sisters at fault, but I guess since I was the oldest of the five, that would be hard to prove. Grasping at straws, I blamed it on my friends and my social environment for steering me to that dismal sickness. But in retrospect, I don't exactly think I was a role model that anyone would want to show off to their children, either. So it looks like I can pin that whole problem on me. No matter; I had other things to do to keep me busy.

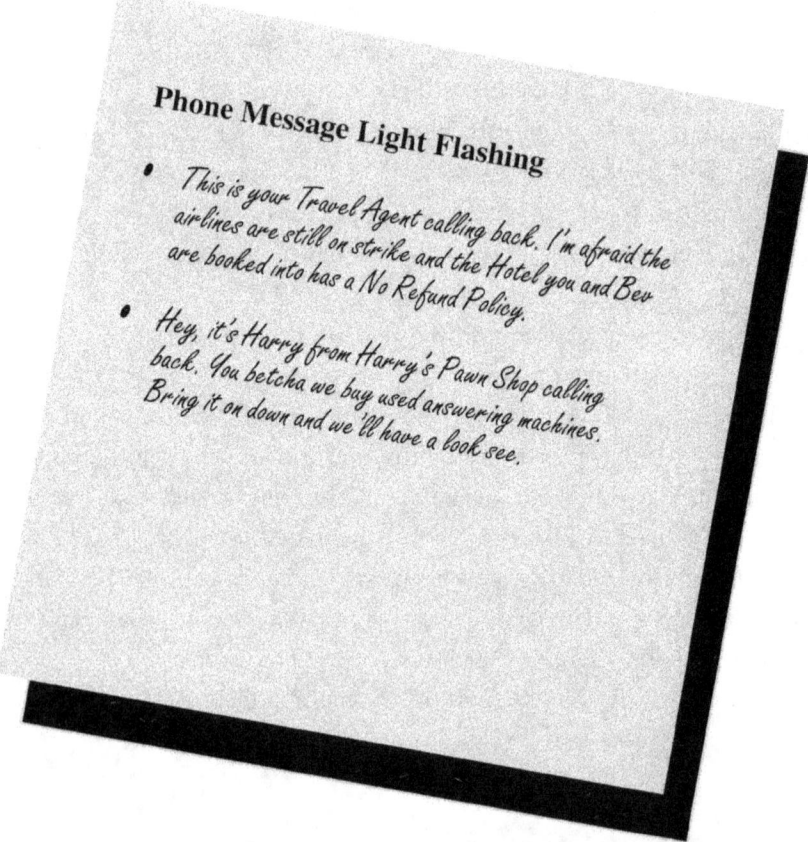

Phone Message Light Flashing

- This is your Travel Agent calling back. I'm afraid the airlines are still on strike and the Hotel you and Bev are booked into has a No Refund Policy.

- Hey, it's Harry from Harry's Pawn Shop calling back. You betcha we buy used answering machines. Bring it on down and we'll have a look see.

Chapter 87

Things To Do List

When everything is going right, that's when I worry the most. First, because that doesn't usually happen and, second, because it gives me a chance to think and worry about everything instead of being too busy to realize what's going on around me. I work better under complete chaos.

This brings up the subject of vacations, because vacations are the same. "Vacation" is the only word in my dictionary that Oxford got completely wrong. The one thing that they really got right was the word "vacate," which comes just prior to their ridiculous definition of "vacation." Oxford states that a "vacation" is a "fixed period of cessation from work." Oh yeah, and they cross-reference the word "holiday," which is all wrong too, to a "day of festivity or recreation, when no work is done." I mean, how far off can you be?

Here's the Landlord's definition of vacation: "A fixed point in time when all chaos will assemble and stay until such said fixed time discontinues." The definition of "holiday" is pretty much the same, except it has the word "insanity" in it.

So my vacation consists of a "Things To Do" list that stays attached to my body until the vacation is over. Here's a typical one:
- Fix appliance in 208A.
- Look at fallen fence. Don't bring tools.
- Clean up broken beer bottles in front of tenant's door.
- Buy beer and steaks.
- Get propane for BBQ.
- Camp out and try to catch 210A for last month's rent.

What really happened? Well, the tenant with the broken appliance wasn't at the suite like they promised. Darned if I was going in by myself. If they found anything missing during the next ten years, I'd get blamed for it.

I knew I didn't need any tools for the broken fence. What I needed was a tractor to push it up straight and fifty tons of concrete to keep it that way. This item just didn't ever seem to fall off my To Do list. I cleaned up the broken glass and I didn't cut myself. Bonus.

Beer and steaks was pretty much a natural. Bring in twelve empties, take out twelve full. Steaks just needed to be more than an inch thick and smaller than the BBQ grill. Properly planned, there should be just enough steak left over to go with my eggs in the morning.

I always topped up the propane. Far too many steaks had ended up half-cooked.

The big project for the day was to track down a tenant who still owed me the rent. I camped out in the driveway until the two beers I had brought were gone, and then I decided to go to Plan B. I left a note on the door and went home.

While I was waiting for him I got so bored I made up a couple of Knock-Knock jokes just to pass the time. They seemed to put the moment into perspective:

Knock-Knock
Who's there?
Tenants.
Tenants who?
Ten ants, good. I need ten ants to start my new ant farm.

Knock-Knock
Who's there?
Fred.

Fred who?

Fred, the Landlord. I'm here to get the rent.

Hello, I said it's Fred and I'm here to get the rent. Can you hear me?

Come on, I know you're in there. You said, "Fred who?" Open up the door.

Stupid Knock-Knock jokes!

Anyway, sure enough, I found out that he just took off in the middle of the night. When I inspected the suite, I noticed a phone number pinned to the bulletin board. I decided to phone and see what I got. A receptionist for a company answered and I asked if my tenant was there. She said, "Sure, would you like to speak to him?" I said no, just give me the address and I'll come and see him.

He sure was surprised to see me. He was really surprised when I said that I would get up on the counter and spread the word quite loudly about how good a tenant he was, and then I would go to his supervisor. Can you believe I got the full month's rent? I sure enjoyed crossing that item off my list.

Most of the time my To Do list just reminds me of the things I didn't do. That's okay, though. At least it makes me look busy.

But Fred (you ask), you must have had some good experiences with a tenant you could tell us about. Actually, I did (thanks for asking).

This really nice lady showed up at one of my suites for rent. She said she was looking at suites for her daughter as she was trying to "motivate" her to move out of the family home. "Fine," I said, "but I really would like your daughter to see the place in person. I prefer to meet my future tenants." She assured me that the suite was fine and so was her daughter.

She wrote me a cheque for two months' rent, including the damage deposit. And it was one of those cheques that didn't have a scenic picture in the background, so I knew it was good. It even had her real name and address on it, which was a first for me.

Well, partway through the month there was no daughter to be seen. Same for the second month. I received another cheque in the mail for the third month. More money, no daughter. Before the fourth month started, I received another cheque with a note stating that the daughter would not be moving in, and I was to keep the damage deposit for the inconvenience. I rented it out to someone else and cashed her cheque.

She was the best tenant I ever had. I'd love to thank her some day, but I don't even know what she looks like.

Chapter 88

The Path to Free Money

It was one of those mornings when I felt like I had donated an organ the night before. I was too scared to plug my phone back in. If there was ever a time for space aliens to beam me up to their mother ship, it was now. The handle of life was broken. A complete lobotomy would have been welcome, unless that was the missing organ from the night before.

When you have the ability to sink this low before eight in the morning, then the day just has to get better. Unfortunately, it didn't work this time; the day just got worse. This adds strength to my theory that God just loves idiots because he made so many of them. I wouldn't mind, except I believe he's sending them all my way for a test drive before releasing them in the wild.

It was raining because it was my day off. Actually, when you're a Landlord there are no days off. Hours of operation are from midnight one day to midnight the next. Believe me, there's lots of activity around the wee hours of the morning.

The letters on my forehead for that day were FM. Not for Fred Miller, no, no, no. They stood for Free Money. Today everyone can have Fred's money. It all started with me getting a free estimate.

"Well, unfortunately, Mr. Miller, it looks bad and unfortunately, it looks like it's going to cost you a lot of money."

"Well, apparently I'll get another quote, and apparently we won't be doing business."

"Well, actually I could use another method and actually drop the price."

"Well, isn't that nice of you. So you mean you don't need access to my bank account?"

Even Bev read the letters on my forehead. I stuck to my usual basic line of questions. "It's very nice, dear, did it cost much?" I asked her.

"Well, if you forget the overseas exchange and shipping charge, it was a steal," she said.

I wondered how many more were on their way. Then I saw the shipping bill. It would have been cheaper to hire a space shuttle from NASA.

"Are the credit cards holding out, dear?"

"Yes, I got them all to raise the spending limits. I'm really looking forward to this new challenge."

"Darn," I thought, "she said the word 'challenge.'" It was project time again. Boy, I hate myself when I get that feeling.

This time I decided I was going to build a path made of slate and concrete. No reason to make a small path. "Go big or go home," was my motto. This baby is going to wrap all the way around the house from the front door to the back.

Now, slate is expensive, so that's why I decided to get my own. There was a mountain up-island about seventy-five miles away that I heard had slate. Somehow I would chisel it out of the side of a mountain. Never done that before. So, keeping in mind that slate weighs a lot and the path was two hundred feet by four feet, I calculated I'd need a gazillion loads of slate and stock options in a gas station, not to mention a truckload of concrete to go with a bargeload of sand from the Sahara Desert. Although I knew this wasn't a six-pack job, I figured it seemed acceptable and put the plan in motion.

So I borrowed a friend's truck but I didn't tell him why I needed it. I don't think he would have liked the idea that I was going up-island to search for a mountain and bring it back with me in his truck. I knew I was going to need big tools for this part of the operation, and I knew I wasn't going to use dynamite. Actually, the idea not to use dynamite came from family and friends, and from some people I didn't even know.

I found the mountain and, lo and behold, I hit it on a good day. It was springtime and the frozen water in between the slate had thawed, and this caused the slate to break away from the mountain. There were chunks of slate lying around everywhere. All I had to do was load enough on to the truck so that the bumper wasn't dragging on the ground. So I kept on going back and forth doing this until most of the mountain was at my place.

Within a month the new walkway was nicknamed the "Pathway From Hell." It was taking far too long and I was bored with mixing concrete, and if I had to make one more trip up-island I'd scream. I tried to imagine just having half a path or a path that gradually tapered from four feet wide down to one foot in width, but it just wasn't working. At the rate I was going, I figured I needed to be reincarnated twice more as myself to finish the job. That would mean going through the Landlord thing all over again, so that wasn't acceptable. I knew I had to get down to basics. It was time to implement Plan B. I was going to throw an all-day, all-you-can-eat-and-drink *Pathway From Hell Party*. The first of its kind!

There were twenty-five of us at the peak of the party. Eight wheelbarrows showed up, and there wasn't a second they didn't have those babies producing concrete. We went through a ton of slate, concrete, pizza and beer, and finished it that day.

Bev and I surveyed the results over a glass of wine just as the sun was going down. We were pleased. Seeing Hormone's paw prints in the concrete didn't even bother us. My "'projecticide" had been cured, and I was good for a while. It was time to get back to the Wacko Land of Landlording.

Chapter 89

Wacko Land

Strange things happen in everyone's life, but if you're a Landlord, you get elevated to a new level where wacko things happen to your life. There are no rules in Wacko Land. Perception number one is that you must have a lot of money. This, of course, is not true. The tenants have all the money, and all you do is try to collect it. Then you give it to the banks. But, because of this perception, everyone figures you must spend your day trying to give your money away to people.

Perception number two is that you must be a big wheeler-dealer if you have a lot of real estate. Yeah right, I still stand in line at McDonald's like everyone else.

Perception number three is that everyone figures you're real smart. Right. Take a look at the scars on my legs from my Robertson screwdriver.

These perceptions are the foundation that Wacko Land is built on.

Like this experience. One day a tenant left a note on my door saying that he didn't have the rent, but he had something much better for me, and that I should "stay tuned." The tenant didn't even sign the note, so I had seven to choose from. Within a few days I had collected all the rent, except from one person who didn't seem to be home. I figured it must be him.

Finally, I got in touch with him. He was very excited as he told me that he had bought an old Mustang car, and I owned half of it with my $800 rent. He was going to do a few improvements to it and then sell it for a profit. I couldn't find him for the next couple of days. I had an eviction notice for him. He ended up finding me. There he was at my doorstep, $1,400 in hand. This, he said, was my half of the investment he had sold that morning. I really loved that Mustang. I hated to see it go.

Income tax is in Wacko Land, but it's more of a zone. Admittedly, I was as dumb as a post when it came to income tax forms. I was an accident waiting to happen. Each year I would pick a new accountant to humiliate me. I, in turn, would leave a garbage bag full of receipts on their desk to sort out. They always had a hissy fit when they saw all my receipts. When it came to answering income tax questions, I plead the Fifth Amendment most of the time (even if it doesn't exist in Canada). No question was too stupid for Fred. I still believe my only two dependents are beer and pizza. Me and income tax were like two ships crashing in the night.

The problem with Wacko Land is that you get used to it. You mention a story to someone who is not familiar with Wacko Land, and they look at you with stunned disbelief. Then you try to explain to them that it's okay; it's normal for Wacko Land. There's not much you can do about it, except buckle up and try not to get sick from the ride.

A good example is watching people move out while someone else moves in. In almost every instance, the people moving out are late and the people moving in are early. The Landlord gets to be the mediator. Usually tempers flare up between the two groups and, for some reason, they all think I'm going to compensate them a gazillion dollars for the inconvenience.

The fact of the matter is there was nothing I could ever do, and I still (usually) hadn't made that month's mortgage payment. So I just sat in the middle of Wacko Land and tried not to get sick.

Usually, right after the new tenant moved in, they would look at me and tell me with a straight face that their couch or their new dining room set doesn't fit. Like somehow they thought it was my problem. Sometimes I told them that I was already planning to knock out a wall, and sometimes I told them I could make it fit; all I had to do was get my chainsaw. Either way, my brain was still in Wacko Land, and I was trying to figure out what grade they were in when they decided to drop out.

Sometimes I wondered what color the sky was in their world.

It's not like all this didn't have an effect on me, either. I was starting to think "Space Unit" was meant to be my real name at birth. It would at least help to explain a lot of things. For instance, the other day I was opening up a can of tomato sauce for my Bankers Pasta dish. Naturally, the cat heard the can opener and came into the kitchen screaming for food. I guess I had my space suit on at the time because I just poured the sauce into the cat's dish, thinking it all connected somehow. Both of us just stared at the sauce, not saying much. Cats don't normally have much in the way of facial expressions, but Hormone definitely had a confused look on his face.

You'd think that would be the end of it, but no, I had to knock a glass off the counter that hit the cat's dish at the perfect angle to get the best possible coverage of sauce imaginable all over the kitchen. Hormone wasn't fast enough to get out of the way, so he immediately transported a healthy portion of the sauce into the living room.

I had difficulty that night explaining to Bev about the red kitty paw tracks throughout the house. I told her this was normal for Wacko Land. Plus, my space suit needed drycleaning.

Each day Wacko Land brings on another thrilling surprise. It kind of feels like a salmon swimming upstream. Everything just keeps pushing you back, and all you can do is keep trying to move forward, bit by bit. All that work, just so that you can get to the very end and die anyway.

Today's surprise came in the form of a truck. I got a call from one of my tenants at the up-and-down duplex who told me most of my fence was gone because a truck drove through it.

"Where's the truck?" I asked.

"Oh, it's gone now," replied the tenant. "We all sat on his tailgate so he could get more traction and his wheels wouldn't spin as much when he was backing his truck up on your lawn."

"Did you get the license number?" I asked.

"No, should I have?"

My insurance agent came by with my file. It took up all the space in his briefcase. I pointed to where I wanted my new fence, but I don't think he was listening. He pointed out to me that it was a very old fence, and then I pointed out to him that I wanted my new fence stained the same color as the one in the back. Neither one of us seemed to be pointing in the same direction.

In the end, they just gave me a cheque, and I got by just fine without a fence. It was a very old fence anyway. So you can see what happens if you don't buckle up when you're in Wacko Land. All I ask for is just one day to be normal, just one day.

That's all I ask.

Chapter 90

Moving On... Again

Bev told me to hurry up and finish dinner. "I'll be waiting in the car," she said. "We have a 7:00 appointment to see a house that's for sale."

Somewhere in that statement I was missing something. Usually the decision to sell your existing house and move for whatever reason is discussed prior to starting to house-hunt. There wasn't anything wrong with the house we were in. I quite liked it, actually, and I didn't see any reason to move. Or maybe we had discussed it and I didn't remember.

"I'll be there in a minute, dear." Unfortunately, Bev liked the house we saw. That led to more houses the next day, and three more the following. This thing was not going to go away. I still didn't remember discussing this move, but I didn't think it mattered anymore. We were going to move and I might as well get on the train before it left the station without me.

After looking at a couple dozen houses, I started to get the same old question from the Real Estate Agent: "Well, what do you want?"

I kept on giving the same clueless answer: "I don't know. I'll know it when I see it." I mean, come on, I haven't had much time to get a reality check on this whole thing. I just got on the train. That doesn't mean I know where it's going yet. Ask Bev; she bought the tickets. I'm just along for the ride.

Well, finally something positive happened. We saw a house that we didn't like, but we fell in love with the street. Half the houses on the street were on the waterfront, and the other half at least had views of the water. I told the Real Estate Agent who had listed the house that I loved the street, hated the house. He told us that if we were serious about the street, he would find us a house on it. I asked him how he intended to do that. He said, "Easy; I live on this street and I know everyone on it. I'll go door to door and find someone willing to sell." We told him to fill his boots.

Two days later he had a house, with an appointment that evening to see it. We showed up early. It was a large house right on the water. It was also a dive. There was so much garbage on the property that we were ready to turn around and leave. But the Real Estate Agent showed up then, so we felt obliged to see it. Much to our surprise, the inside was spectacular. They had just finished spending $85,000 on installing a gourmet kitchen alone.

But we couldn't get over the outside mess. Apparently the owner was a pack rat and would grab anything that floated by his house. Suddenly I saw the potential through the horrific landscaping and the garbage. This place could be salvaged. I tried to get Bev to see the vision. She couldn't see it, nor did she want to. She wanted to go.

"Look," I said, "it has a hundred and forty-three feet of waterfront."

"Where?" she said. "I don't see it."

To make a long story short, I told Bev to trust me. We bought the place for $359,000. Normally, I'd tell you the story of trying to get more money from the bank to buy this place. Especially with my bank account showing a negative balance. But I think you get the picture by now.

Chapter 91

Sold

In order to buy the new house, we had to sell the old one. We gave the listing to the same agent who sold it to us in the first place. I told her I wanted $220,000 for the place. She argued that I had only paid $120,000 for it three years ago, and that I just wouldn't get that kind of money. I told her that the five appliances in the garage were part of the deal, as well as the Pathway From Hell. And let's not forget the ferry dock on the side of the house that we called a sun deck. She said I still wouldn't get that kind of money.

Two days later it sold for $220,000. I paid $10,600 in commissions to the Real Estate Agent. Not bad money for two flippin' days work. (Refer to recipe in Chapter 74, Stuffed Real E-Steak in a Rich and Heavy Cream Sauce.)

We moved into the new place. The former owner promised to remove the stuff that was littered all over the yard. He took about ten truckloads away, and then I never saw him again. I followed up with another five truckloads to the dump. I was finally starting to see patches of green.

When I finally got a chance to survey the place, I realized that it was going to need that magic touch that only my tools knew how to produce. There were the usual projects that made most of my body parts previously associated with past projects cringe. But there were new ones that I envisioned. Ones that put me in a confused yet eager state of euphoria. Like building a dock and a three-tiered cascading waterfall, along with retaining walls down by the shore so I could put in a sandy beach. I figured a sandy beach was important, so I had two truckloads of sand delivered right away. (Hormone was in heaven when he saw that giant kitty litter mountain. It sure made him popular with the other cats on the street!)

I didn't know how to tackle any of these new projects (like you didn't already have that one figured out), but they say "nothing ventured, nothing gained" or, as my battle cry goes, "nothing fractured, nothing maimed!" (Actually, it was my insurance company that introduced me to that motto.)

Anyway, I was in project heaven, and I was the man to do this for two reasons. First, there was no money to contract any of this out, and second, my insurance policy was up to date.

With Hormone supervising from the top of his kitty mountain, I proceeded with the first project. I needed about fifty boulders all weighing about two tons each, and about forty yards of dirt. I was going to build a retaining wall so that my property line would stop shrinking every time the tide changed. Since I can only lift a hundred pounds at a time, I decided to break reason number one and contract out most of the project, thereby keeping me from making a claim under reason number two. I remember I had to sign something at the bank to finance reason number one. I also remember when they pulled my file out at the bank, it was so thick that they realized it wasn't worth their while trying to figure out if I qualified or not. All I know is that I had another account to "balance," and I use the word "balance" very loosely.

The retaining wall went in just fine. The contractor was a little agitated that he had to work around the mountain of sand that was in his way, but it was Hormone's mountain now, not mine. When I finally did get all the sand down to the shore to make a beach, it was twenty percent kitty poop. I did the environmentally right thing and raked it all up, but you could see that Hormone was a bit confused because he already had it perfectly buried until I came along and wrecked everything. He wouldn't sit on my lap for weeks after that episode.

Next project was the waterfall. That meant more boulders. This project was more exciting because it involved my favorite playthings like electricity, plumbing and concrete. I knew I'd need a lot more sand to mix with the cement, so I got another truckload delivered. I was back in Hormone's good books.

If you've never built a waterfall going into a pond, you should try. There's no reason for me to be the only one getting stressed out around here. The bottom line is that ponds leak, and continue to leak until you decide to move away. I even put fish in the pond. Now all the seagulls are hanging around, waiting for me to put another batch in. Dumb project. Stupid pond.

Next project was building a patio of interlocking bricks. Heck if I was going to use concrete and slate, and do that mountain thing again. This patio required "accuracy" because it linked two outside sliding glass doors together, and also wound around to connect with the shed. That meant I had to use the words "level" and "grade" in my design. I knew the bricks had no intention of fitting in according to my plan, and that some of them would have to be "cut" in order for them to fit properly. I don't like the words "level," "grade," "cut" or "accuracy" when it comes to putting a plan together. I'm just shooting for the phrase, "I'm done, honey, can I have a beer now?"

Well, to make a long story short, halfway through I got tired of the project. ("Level" wasn't happening, and "cut" was around the corner.) That happened to coincide with my brother Ken needing to borrow $700 for this guitar he just HAD to have. Just how bad did Ken want the guitar? Bad enough to finish the patio off, that's how bad.

Chapter 92

Send in Substitute Landlord #2

Chris was our tenant in the new house. (Of course I had an illegal suite. What were you thinking?) And he thought the idea of being the new Substitute Landlord and taking care of business would be good. And, of course, he would get paid for it. For myself, I had passed on a headache and gained a tax deduction.

Chris was naive at first. He didn't know about the Secret Handbook. The other tenants I had at the time were very experienced with the handbook. As they started applying the contents of the handbook to the new rookie I, in turn, would coach Chris with the available options. It was tenant vs. tenant for a change.

One day, Chris got the same old letter from the Tenancy Branch for his arbitration hearing. He was in the midst of a dispute with one of the tenants over the amount being held back from his damage deposit. Chris had charged him $50 for work he had done to get the suite back to normal. I told Chris that since the $50 went in his pocket for his work, then this was his arbitration hearing. Besides, he didn't need to know my batting average.

I had a sudden premonition: Chris was going to win this one. I told him to make sure he told the arbitrator that he was not the Landlord. "They're not out to get you, Chris, they're after me," I said. Sure enough, Chris won. Go figure.

I started to notice Chris using unhealthy four-letter words. The timing coincided with Bev's learning curve. I asked him how things were going, and he said everything was f#@*ing fine, so I left it at that.

About a year later Chris had had enough. He begged to become a normal tenant again. Sure, why not? Bev and I were refreshed and ready to get back in the ring. But then I noticed Chris was drinking a lot more than usual.

It was good while it lasted.

Chapter 93

Another Day... Again

Why was everyone raining on my parade? My morning started off with my egg exploding in the microwave, followed by my bread catching fire in the toaster oven. My car wouldn't start, but it didn't matter anyway, because the tire went flat overnight and the bolt holding down the spare had snapped off. I was having a bad hair day and my nose was peeling from a sunburn from the day before. There was no beer in the fridge, and the cat threw up on the center of the rug.

Normally, I would have just turned around and gone back to bed, but there was a spring sticking up in the middle of the mattress that never gave me a good sleep anyway. The phone was ringing, and the coffee managed to miss the opportunity to successfully drip into the pot. Instead, the counter and the kitchen floor were having coffee that morning. There was no coffee left for me to have while reading the morning paper, which didn't come anyway. By now, it should have started to rain. At least that might have helped the hundreds of bulbs in the garden to get their act in gear.

Little did I know that my bad day hadn't even started yet. The phone call I mentioned? One of my suites had flooded because one of the tenants had left the sprinkler on all night. The ground became so saturated with water that it seeped through the concrete and drywall into the living room. Like I was going to tell my insurance agency that I had another flood.

I had to borrow my neighbor's car to check out the suite. When I returned the car to my neighbor after topping up the gas, he pointed to a dent in the side of the car. I told him that it matched all the other dents in the car. He pointed once again and called it "my" dent. Later, I got to buy "my" dent for $150.

It was a pathetic day, and it wasn't ten in the morning yet. The paper finally arrived. Normally, I would have been eating a muffin while reading the paper, but that was still sitting on a countertop at the gas station. Paid for, naturally. The cat was screaming at me because it was hungry. The stupid thing wouldn't have been hungry if it hadn't puked up all its food on the rug. I noticed another tire on my car was slowly going flat. I couldn't get to the bank to borrow money from my credit line to pay for all of this.

It turned 11:00. I was humbled, broke and hungry. "I'm going to put my mind to work on this," I thought to myself. The day got worse. I sprained my ankle stepping on one of the shovels I had borrowed from my neighbor. The same neighbor with "my" dent in his car. I immediately thought lawsuit.

Like he's going to see that shovel again.

A new word started to surface in my vocabulary. It all started with words like what's the "chance" of this happening or could that "possibly" happen to me again? Then it became clear that it all fell under the big umbrella word, "probability." It was starting to change how I looked at things. Now, you don't have to be a mathematician or goat herder to realize that if you just stop long enough to apply your experience to the next upcoming situation, you have a better chance of shaping the outcome or "probability" in your favor. For instance:

Example #1: One tenant was never home at the beginning of the month when the rent was due. (Or else he just did a good job of hiding behind the couch all day.) So the day before the rent was due I knocked on the door. Sure he was home; it wasn't rent day. Well, we discussed tomorrow's rent pickup so that the "probability" of me getting my rent would greatly increase. Lo and behold, I got my rent, as agreed. (Of course, that was the last time he was ever home again the day before rent was due.)

Example #2: Go out and buy an expensive gift for Bev. She's going to do it anyway, so I figure I might just as well get in the good books for buying it. (Plus, I don't have to explain why I'm filling the fridge up with beer again.)

Example #3: Tell the bank you can get a better rate somewhere else. You'll get a better rate.

So, in the end, I designed my own Tenant Rental Application Form in the hopes that the "probability" of getting a good tenant would be increased.

Tenant Rental Application Form

MULTIPLE CHOICES (that means pick one or more)

Question 1: *Why do you want to rent this suite?*
A) The Landlord looks like he has never seen the Tenants' Secret Handbook.
B) Because I got kicked out of my last place for not paying the rent.
C) It looks like I can store my three cars here until I get them on the road again.
D) I just broke out of prison and I need a place real quick.

Question 2: *A damage deposit is for:*
A) The Landlord to invest in mutual funds on my behalf.
B) Letting me party in your $200,000 house.
C) The last half-month's rent when I leave this dump.
D) Nothing, because I'll get it all back through the Tenancy Branch if I have to.

Question 3: *Rent is due:*
A) When the Landlord finds me.
B) When all the other bills have been paid.
C) After the first cheque bounces.
D) After I've used at least three excuses from the Tenants' Secret Handbook.

Question 4: *I will adhere to the Landlord/Tenant Agreement:*
A) If you can prove in court that that's my signature.
B) Only if the Supreme Court of Canada rules in your favor.
C) Until my biker friends get here.
D) If it's a life or death situation and we're not talking about MY life or death.

Question 5: *You will offer to cut the lawn when:*
A) I know the lawn mower is broken.
B) The Landlord just finished doing it.
C) There is a sizable stack of money involved for doing it.
D) Hell freezes over.

Question 6: *You will offer the Landlord a beer when:*
A) Your rent money has been spent on beer.
B) You have seriously broken something.
C) You want to introduce me to your new pets.
D) This is a trick question.

Tenant Rental Application Form, Page 2

Question 7: *You need me to come right over because:*
A) You want to see if my insurance covers this.
B) I won't believe what happened when you forgot to turn the oven off this morning.
C) You've locked yourself out.
D) The firemen want to talk to me.

Question 8: *Rent is not paid when:*
A) The bank screwed up your accounts again.
B) Aunt Agnes in Texas died again.
C) I wasn't there when you had the money.
D) I left it in your mailbox. Didn't you get it?

Question 9: *You know you said you would do it, but:*
A) It's my Aunt Agnes in Texas again.
B) My favorite TV show was on and I plumb forgot.
C) I thought you would probably do a better job.
D) I spent the money you lent me on something else so I'll do it when I get paid next month.

Question 10: *My dog will stop barking when:*
A) He feels like it.
B) He eats another Landlord.
C) He's allowed to finish chewing all of the outside cables to the house.
D) All of the above.

Question 11: *My car will stop leaking oil on your driveway when:*
A) The Landlord fixes it.
B) An Act of God fixes it.
C) I sell my other two cars first and then sell this one.
D) All the oil eventually leaks out.

Question 12: *When things break:*
A) It's not my fault.
B) The Landlord has lots of insurance.
C) It was already broken when I got here.
D) It's a reason not to pay rent.

Tenant Rental Application Form, Page 3

Question 13: *I will purchase a second or third vehicle:*
A) With the rent money.
B) If there is no place to park it, which is now the Landlord's problem.
C) If it's under $100 and needs a little work.
D) To keep up with the other tenants.

Question 14: *Tenant emergencies happen:*
A) Between midnight and six in the morning.
B) When the Landlord sits down for dinner.
C) On a Sunday when the hardware store is closed.
D) When I try to fix something.

Question 15: *The window broke because:*
A) El Nino did it.
B) Atmospheric pressure did it.
C) The Earth's tectonic plates shifted last night.
D) A small asteroid hit it and then disintegrated, causing that burn on the rug.

Question 16: *An obvious reason to phone the Landlord is when:*
A) You've plugged up the toilet and lost the instructions on how the plunger works.
B) The water level in the suite doesn't seem to be going down.
C) You would rather settle out of court.
D) You have to explain why the police will be contacting me.

Question 17: *Yes, I realize you're the Landlord, but:*
A) You have my deposit, therefore I own you.
B) This is now my place and I have my own Branch totally dedicated to keeping it that way.
C) Everyone grows pot in their suite.
D) We're going to do it my way, okay?

Question 18: *If you know for certain your damage deposit will not cover last night's damage from the party you had, you will:*
A) Have another party, only bigger next time.
B) Sell the light fixtures at the next party.
C) Turn the double-pane glass windows into single panes to help absorb the loss.
D) Call it a plant party and dig up the Landlord's garden plants for your next place.

Tenant Rental Application Form, Page 4

Question 19: Assuming you are planning on buying the Landlord's property, you will:
A) Ask for a reduction in rent to help achieve your goals.
B) Offer to throw in your three vehicles in order to create a partnership.
C) Offer to put the light fixtures and window panes back as a gesture of good will.
D) Offer lots of beer and just hope he signs.

Question 20: If the tenant next door is having a loud party you will:
A) Phone the Landlord to complain and then join the party.
B) Phone the Landlord and threaten to phone City Hall about the illegal suite if he doesn't solve the problem immediately.
C) Phone the police and give them the Landlord's address and phone number.
D) Complain to the Landlord, the police, City Hall, and then join the party.

Question 21: If you detect a water leak in the building, you will:
A) Assume it will go away.
B) Refuse to pay the water bill.
C) Stop paying rent and call your lawyer.
D) Notify the landlord if the building shifts or starts sinking.

Question 22: I'm giving you one month's notice because:
A) I'm leaving in one week.
B) You keep hassling me about paying the rent, so now I'm not paying anything!
C) My damage deposit isn't going to cover this thing I have to show you.
D) I'm going to go live with Aunt Agnes in Texas.

The good thing about this form is that there are no wrong answers. It's just a matter of renting to the tenant who checks off the least number of answers.

Application to be a Landlord

BEFORE YOU FILL OUT THE APPLICATION TO BE A LANDLORD, WE ASSUME YOU KNOW THAT:

- You have no life
- You don't know how to invest your money properly in anything else (or you would have already)
- You are prepared to loan out your property, valued at approximately $200,000, secured only by a $500 damage deposit (that's a 400-to-1 ratio; think Las Vegas)
- There is no Landlord Branch (but the tenants have one)
- Your new branch is Revenue Canada (and they are looking forward to meeting you)
- Tenants can run and hide (you can't)
- They can write bad cheques (you can't)
- You must pay the mortgage (maybe they'll pay the rent)
- You pay property taxes and capital gains (they don't)
- You buy insurance and pay school taxes (they send their kids to school using your taxes and sue you when the time is right, using your insurance policy)
- All repairs to your property will cost a lot and consume your life
- You may have to migrate to Africa when it's over

IF YOU STILL WANT TO FILL OUT THE APPLICATION TO BE A LANDLORD, WE MUST GET A DOCTOR'S APPROVAL FROM A QUALIFIED PSYCHIATRIST. AND PLEASE, ONCE YOU'RE A LANDLORD, BOOK SOME FUTURE APPOINTMENTS WITH THE PSYCHIATRIST WHILE YOU STILL HAVE AN OUNCE OF BRAIN LEFT.

Please circle T for True and F for False.
This questionnaire is for the general public.
Watch out: there are two trick questions.

1.	If an appliance breaks, the Landlord will be there in five minutes, haul it away on his back, and return it fixed within ten minutes.	T	F
2.	If you do not have the rent, the Landlord will cover for you up to three months.	T	F
3.	The Landlord is a billionaire and this is just a hobby.	T	F
4.	To get a job at Revenue Canada you must be a meat eater and have a good arm for throwing darts.	T	F
5.	You believe this statement: "Once money is deposited in a bank, technically it is now their money to spend."	T	F
6.	Scotch (not beer) will temporarily solve Capital Gains problems with Revenue Canada.	T	F
7.	The Tenancy Branch is an unbiased arbitrator who can help you drive the golf ball further.	T	F
8.	You should take motion sickness pills if you visit Wacko Land.	T	F
9.	Up until now, it is only a scientific theory that it can rain indoors.	T	F
10.	If your daughter is missing her hairbrush and she is now leaving the house with her hair conditioner, she is effectively giving you one week's notice that she's moving out.	T	F
11.	You can learn cooking at Landlord School.	T	F
12.	City Hall provides a nonprofit lawn cutting service.	T	F
13.	Illegal suites are only illegal if they look illegal.	T	F
14.	Substitute Landlords have a life expectancy of one year.	T	F
15.	Football, when mixed with marriage, has a life expectancy of about half a season.	T	F
16.	The best tools are neighbors' tools.	T	F

Some helpful hints if you're having trouble:

Question 3: If you answered True, please go back to Chapter 1 and start all over. You just don't get it.

Question 5: If you answered True, you can get a job as a Bank Manager. If you answered False, you can get a job as an Assistant Bank Manager.

Question 6: This is somewhat of a trick question because I didn't mention how MUCH Scotch it would take to solve the Problem. Actually, there's a simple formula you can apply to this issue. For every $1,000 paid to Revenue Canada for Capital Gains, just multiply it by one bottle of Scotch. The mathematical formula is: $1(S) \times (CG/1,000) = P$ (this is a perfect wallet-size version).

Question 7: This is a trick question. It is both true and false, so you got one right for sure.

Question 8: This is a trick question. Don't go to Wacko Land is the correct answer.

Question 9: To test this theory, insert the plug in your sink and turn the water on full for three-and-a-half hours. Then call your insurance company to confirm the results. (Putting a few dishes in the sink is optional and will not affect the test results.)

Question 10: Refer to Chapter 41 for the answer.

Question 13: Think "stove."

Question 14: Ask Bev or Chris.

Question 15: Ladies, if you answered NO to this question, get in touch with Bev for her free brochure outlining her twelve-easy-step program on *How to Deflate His Pigskin During Halftime*.

Question 16: Read this another way. The ONLY tools are neighbors' tools. That should help.

Anyway, enough tests. Back to the situation at hand.

Chapter 97

Deep Thoughts

Well, on the good side of things, I never had a fire in any of my places. I had so many instances of water damage that a fire wouldn't stand a chance. On the bad side of things, I got to know my insurance agent much better than I wanted.

Another good thing is I never went berserk and killed anyone. It's not that I didn't picture the people from Revenue Canada, for instance, dangling by their thumbs. It's just that I figure everybody has a place in the food chain, and you can't eliminate a whole species of bottom feeders without upsetting the balance somewhere. Some people call it "life's little lessons." I call it "battle scars."

I mean, one day I got a call from a tenant who asked me if it was OK to poke a hole in one of the walls so he could fit his new stereo in. Of course not, you silly person. But he really tried hard to convince me that it would be OK, even though I insisted it would not happen. When the day came about a year later for him to move out, I inspected the place. I saw a poster of a cat taped to the wall. I asked him the two obvious questions: "Why aren't you taking your poster, and why is it so low to the ground?"

I got the obvious answer of, "It's for my cat to look at" and, "You can keep the poster if you want to." The "wall" request came to mind, and I calmly went over and poked my finger through the poster into the gash in the wall.

I just stood there wondering why he thought I was so stupid, and then the Tenancy Branch flashed before my eyes. I wondered if they had some kind of stereo-widening clause that allowed him to do that. We agreed to donate his damage deposit to a drywaller. Later that day I was off to another suite. I was eating pizza out of the box while I was driving along and then, all of a sudden, I realized my life was like a double-anchovy pizza, and it wasn't a 2-for-1 special, that's for sure.

I'm not a symbolic type of guy, but the slices were disappearing fast (in other words, *life was getting shorter*); the anchovies were overpowering the rest of the flavors (*life was becoming all Landlording*); and I wasn't sharing it with anyone else (*we're talking family values here*). Added to that, I was eating it out of the box (*I wasn't home much*). It was definitely time for a change. I'd get Chinese take-out next time.

Chapter 98

Fred's Gumbo Soup

I had only one thought: this Landlord thing better make me financially independent one day. It would be kind of nice if I stayed sane so that I knew I was enjoying my financial independence. It would be kind of nice, too, if my wife didn't leave me by then either. If I could hang on to my good health, that would be a bonus.

It was a real shame that I missed Sam's first kindergarten Christmas concert at school. Not much I could have done. It was a real emergency at one of the suites. I think my priorities are all messed up! Sometimes I overrate my presence in the world. Like I personally made those interest rates rise, and I drove up the price of appliances with my arsenal of electricity-sucking machines. I figure my taxes are so high that I should have had at least one road named after me. I've paid so much money for school taxes that Sammy should have his own school by now.

Sometimes I think that if I don't rent this suite out to this tenant, then the next one who comes along will be a better fabricator of the facts with more skeletons in the closet, and I'll end up renting to them. That's if there is another one to even show up.

I've been told that my body parts are only worth a couple of bucks when I die. (Like someone's going to buy them.) Scientists attest to the fact that my brain capacity is way under-utilized. I haven't evolved as much as I think. Actually, as a Landlord I feel sometimes that I've evolved into a much lower life form. On the plus side, I make a good omelet, now that Bev forced me to buy a frying pan. I've evolved from steaks to chicken, but that scenario scares me a bit. I still don't bake anything, so I'm proud of that.

My presence on this Earth will be totally unnoticed in about twenty years. A million beers and pizzas will have been purchased and still gone unnoticed. I definitely overrate my presence in the world because, in the end, I'm really nothing more than Fred's Gumbo Soup. Except in my world of Gumbo Soup, I've added a heavy dose of perseverance. It is now the main ingredient for life as I know it. You see, everyone wanted a taste of Fred, but there was no way they were going to get their hands into my soup!

My bank wanted to charge me $185 to renew my mortgage with them at a HIGHER interest rate than the last one!

The property assessment from the City on my two rental places was UP almost forty percent. That meant forty percent MORE in property taxes. My house assessment went up sixty-five percent!

My house insurance for all three properties went UP twenty-five percent.

I was looking at some pretty big bucks getting ready to make an exit from my skinny little wallet, but what they didn't know was, I had adopted *perseverance* and, boy, am I annoying when I get like that.

I challenged the City, the Insurance Company and the Bank. I was like a bull terrier hanging onto their pants with my teeth. I wouldn't let go, no matter what. No one had a supervisor I didn't get to. I fired off a letter to every department, and there wasn't a Manager who didn't get my attention. I was being a total jerk.

In the end, they lowered my assessments on the rental properties by ten percent and my house by twenty-five percent. I changed Insurance Companies and saved a bundle. The Bank gave me a better mortgage rate and dropped the $185 renewal fee after I threatened to leave them for the first bank that would give me a free toaster if I moved my account over.

I wasn't very popular with any of them when it was all over, but hey, I figured I had the same chance of getting invited over to their place for dinner as I did before, so no skin off my chicken.

Why is it that I feel like I'm in some kind of war zone? What the heck am I doing here? It was time to look at my life. It was time to sell the properties and *get* a life. But first, I needed to do some soul-searching.

I asked Bev if she could take care of things for a day. I needed time to think. She said, "Sure, just give me a minute to change."

Chapter 99

Salmon and Soul-Searching

Today's goal was to just hide from everyone and search my soul for the right decision on whether to sell or not. So I went salmon fishing with Sam and my brother Ken. Ken said the fish only bite in the morning. "I don't care," I told him. "We stay out here until dark or until the beer is gone, whichever comes first."

I had two basic strategies for a successful one-day hideout. Don't get the fishhook caught on anyone was the first. And the second was, don't fall overboard because the water is deep and cold and I don't breathe water very well.

I used smelly bait. That wasn't the original plan, but that's what happens when you leave it on the counter overnight. My theory was, how else would the fish know it was there? I've got to believe that they don't hear that well (ever seen fish ears?), so their other senses are heightened, seeing as they only have four left. Keeping in mind that salt water probably hurts their eyes like it does mine, I figured their sense of smell must be keen.

Catching fish would have been just a bonus but, believe it or not, we caught four. That didn't mean we were smart fishermen or that the fish were dumb or anything, as long as the fishes' IQ didn't affect the flavor. It's not like we saved a lot of money, either, by catching them ourselves instead of buying them at the supermarket. Gas was around $35 for cruising all day, and the beer cost twice that much for drinking all day. Fishing is the only sport where a beer tastes good before six in the morning. Anyway, the fish were off to the BBQ. Write me for a fabulous black bean sauce on BBQ'd salmon.

In between catching fish, I happened to glance over at this *Guidebook on Salmon Fishing* that was sitting on top of the tackle box. As I was flipping through the book, I started to realize catching fish was a lot like catching rent. Like, tell me these similarities don't run shivers down your spine?

You have to be there at the right time of day when the fish (tenants) are biting, or you'll never catch them. Very early in the morning seems to work for both. You have to make sure your boat (car) is not too loud as you approach, or you'll scare them off before you even get there. If you don't use the right bait (pay up or get evicted), you'll never catch them. Even if you hook them (get a cheque), that doesn't mean you've caught anything yet. You still have to land them in the boat (clear the cheque through the bank). Of course, there is the catch and release program where you actually get the cheque in the boat, but the cheque bounces, and the tenant skips out during the night.

How about when you get your hook caught on the bottom? You yank and pull and scream, and it doesn't matter how many times you circle around the snag, because you soon realize that something's going to break and it's probably not going to be that thing on the bottom you're caught up on. That pretty much sums up the old Eviction Notice period.

And what about those "postdated cheques"? That's the same as trolling around for hours all day and getting nothing. They both have the same result. Or how about getting just part of the rent? Same as catching a Ling cod and someone says, "It'll be fine as long as you put a lot of lemon on it." I was fishing for salmon, not cod, you dumb halibut!

Then there's the trolling around to collect the rent, and just when you get a little tug on the line and you think you've caught something, all you pull up to the side of the boat is seaweed on the end of your hook. After that happens several times, what Secret Handbook springs to mind? I mean, that is the guts of the book, isn't it? To delay the paying of rent by fooling the fisherman.

Makes sense too that they hang around in schools (comparing Tenants' Handbook notes), and they're too deep for us to see them to figure out what's going on. You need a depth finder to find one, and you have to look in the window to find the other.

And even after you finally net the fish, it still fights and slashes around in the boat, getting all tangled up in your net and making a bloody mess. You never seem to get the rent without a big fight in the end. Plus, rent never gets delivered to your door. I mean, that would be like a fish jumping into your boat, wouldn't it? It just never happens!

And, of course, don't forget you'd better be legal about all this (especially when you're clubbing the fish). Don't forget the Wildlife Officers (Tenancy Branch) are out there. And I'll tell you this, it's not the fish they're looking to scale!

When the day is all over, you get back on dry land and your sea legs are all wobbly from spending all day trying to catch fish (rent). You reflect on the catch limit for the day and you realize that, once again, you never got your quota. You've got to go out again.

Anyway, after catching these four fish that now looked like rent cheques, I thought about selling the properties. But I didn't really know which way to turn. I didn't normally talk to God very much. Nature was all around me, but stepping on a slug was about as close as I got to it. I didn't read books. Can't really say I was well-rounded intellectually, but I had never had an inclination to stay in a mental ward either, so I guess I was technically stable. Either that, or life had me on "pause" or "mute" for the time being. That's OK as long as they tell me when they're going to change the channel.

That's when I realized it was time for **me** to change channels. I was tired of watching this program. It was time to sell!

After deciding to sell, I did an instant flashback. You see, through all of this I have two sisters, Terri and Heather. With my two brothers, Dan and Ken, we make quite the set of siblings. We're all married and I think we've managed to generate about fifteen grandchildren for our parents. We're like a bunch of rabbits, but hey, we inherited that from Mom and Dad.

Anyway, Heather and Terri had only one piece of advice for me through the entire Landlord thing: "Don't be silly, just sell everything." (As opposed to their other motto that worked for everything else: "Don't be silly, just buy it.")

Well, I think after listening to that for twelve years it was finally time to take their advice.

The advice about *selling* that is. I'm still going to be *silly!*

Chapter 100

Going, Going, Gone

It was an incredible feeling coming to the decision to sell both rental properties. It was the only practical solution to saving our sanity. Unfortunately, when we put them up for sale, they didn't sell. Bev was stressed. The Real Estate Agent was upset that I wouldn't change my prices. The tenants were all angry with me for being inconvenienced by all the prospective buyers. Somehow, I had successfully raised the stress levels in the Miller household single-handedly.

Two months after the fourplex was off the market, our Real Estate Agent said, "Let's give it another try at a different price."

"Sure," I said. "Let's give it another try at the same price." He reluctantly agreed, and three days later he sold it for only a few thousand less than the asking price.

I was pleased. I had paid $70,000 for the one side at the beginning. I bought Dan out for $123,000, for a total of $193,000. I sold the place lock, stock and barrel for $384,000. Revenue Canada and the Capital Gains gang were very, very proud of me. The only tiny little glitch was that the possession date was two months away. The agreement was that the new owners could move in and pay rent for two months until they officially took possession. Only two months left, I thought.

What could go wrong?

Chapter 101

Impossible

The new owners (who were now in the top suite) asked my permission to go ahead and replace the linoleum. Hey, you'll own the suites outright in six days, five hours and eighteen minutes. "Go ahead," I said.

They started their prep work, bought the linoleum and, on the very last day that the fourplex was in my name, they decided to move all of their appliances (that were still technically my appliances) into the backyard. Washer, dryer, stove, fridge and dishwasher. They did this so they could lay the linoleum down more easily. Normally you could get away with this, but they didn't factor in the tenants.

A couple of hours later the soon-to-be owners looked out the window to see half the appliances being loaded onto a truck. The police were there in minutes, and so was I. How could this be happening, I thought? It was 6:00 p.m. At midnight (in six hours) the place wasn't even mine anymore. Now the police wanted me to come to the station to press charges and fill out reports. I would have to appear in court to testify.

For some reason, the thieves just didn't look like thieves to me. They kept on telling one officer that they paid for the appliances. They were madly trying to find the receipt. Finally, they did. The officer asked if it was my signature. "No," I said, "but I think I recognize it." Sure enough, it was one of my tenants. My tenant had sold my appliances.

Somehow the tenant thought she was doing me a favor. She thought we were going to throw all those good appliances out. She got $500 for the lot and was quite proud of it. Everybody was laughing but me. So I apologized to the new owners and the police for breaking up the crime ring, and to the thieves who weren't thieves. I told my tenant that in five hours I would not even own the place but, to be on the safe side, I would spend the remaining hours with her. I realized that she wasn't the sharpest knife in the drawer.

You'd think this story was flippin' impossible, wouldn't you?

Chapter 102

Going, Going, Gone... Again

I had the up-and-down duplex on the market for a couple of weeks and, bang, it was gone with no hitches. Hey, the kitchens in both suites were almost new, thanks to the floods and rainfall caused by the tenants. That reminded me that I should send them a Christmas card.

I made a healthy profit. I had bought the unit for $80,900 and sold it for $196,400. I kept thinking what it would have been like if only I had bought ten places back then. I would have been a millionaire. I'd also be dead, I thought.

As quickly as the duplex had become my focal point in life, it was gone again. I think of it now as nothing more than bricks, board and concrete. Oh, and with one great closet organizer and outdoor BBQ.

So it was time to celebrate, eh? Bev and I decided to prepare a gourmet meal that night. Spinach salad with real pan-fried bacon bits, crab cakes, asparagus in white wine sauce, and *Stuffed Real E-Steak* fresh off the BBQ, sliced thin and topped with peppercorn sauce.

I set out plates on the stove element, with the two boiled eggs on top, ready to be sliced up for the salad. Bev went to wash up, and I went to light the candles and freshen our wine for the romantic evening.

The plates exploded into a gazillion pieces because the stove element was still too hot from boiling the eggs. No idea where the two eggs landed, but there were fragments from the plates in every square inch of the kitchen. We had to throw out every piece of food.

Bev ordered a real expensive meal at the restaurant that night.

We found bits of egg and plate fragments throughout the kitchen over the next few months. Bev never hesitated to remind me of my culinary cooking skills throughout that time. I don't think she plans on me living this one down. "Even the tenants were never that stupid," she told me.

So I came up with this good idea on how to get back into Bev's good books. I went out and bought a chainsaw! I thought I would surprise Bev when I explained to her how much money we would save by me going out into the forest all by myself and cutting wood for the fireplace. For some reason she wasn't impressed. She immediately polled all of the people who knew us and asked them if I should be allowed to own a chainsaw. Well, in the end, lucky for me, the store had a "no refund policy," so I got to keep the little baby. (I had already nicknamed it "the big ripper," after Sammy's favorite star constellation.)

The store said I could exchange it for something else, but the only thing I wanted more than a chainsaw was one of those ride-em lawn mowers that you could sit on when you cut the lawn. All I had to do was give the chainsaw back and tack another couple thousand onto the credit card, and everything would be fine. I already had three lawn mowers in the shed, so pretty tough stuff to justify. Besides, Bev just kept picturing me losing control of the thing and driving right off the rock wall and into the water. When I told her this mower came complete with a "refreshment" holder, she knew I was better off with the chainsaw.

Anyway, I proceeded to cut things. It didn't matter what I cut, as long as I got to hear the roar of the engine and got to suck in the fumes of the oil and gas mixture. I was feeling kind of macho with this thing at my side. Should have had one of these when I was dealing with the tenants.

I only ended up using it for a month or so. One day, it just wouldn't start up. Bev looked kind of sad when I told her, but it was hard to tell because she was drinking champagne and orange juice with her friends at some kind of celebration brunch she was having. Not sure what they were celebrating, but no matter, I thought. I'd saved up enough money to buy this used go-cart that Sammy and I saw in the newspaper. She's really going to be impressed when she sees how fast this baby goes. And Sammy doesn't even need a license to drive it! I'll wait until after the party to tell Bev "the good news."

There's no sense in going into any kind of detail concerning "the good news." Sammy and I were going to be go-cartless, according to Bev's new *Accident Prevention Program* that I didn't know anything about. (I assumed it was because Sammy was still too young.)

That's when I decided we needed something altogether different, so I started pricing out boats. Didn't know much about boats, but I didn't need to. Somehow, boats were linked to go-carts that were linked to chainsaws in the ride-em lawn mower category. We were going to be boatless.

In the end, we got a canoe. Bev wouldn't let me get an engine for it, so we got paddles instead. Sammy had to wear so many lifejackets in the canoe, he was as big as me. The family was back on track. I was just waiting for the right time to tell Bev about the large boulders that were going to be delivered for this big water fountain I was going to build. The plan included stacking these boulders up about eight feet high and running water pumps up through the center of them. I guess I'll tell her "the good news" when the boulders get here.

Chapter 103

The Tenants' Secret Handbook... Unplugged

I know it exists, although I still haven't seen one yet. But it's been used on me so many times I pretty well know the contents. They're all cute and pungent, and here they are, in no particular order:

1. It's the first of the month already?

2. I sent the cheque in the mail. Didn't you get it? (This is a good one when they don't even know where you live.)

3. I get paid next Friday. Can you wait until then?

3a. (Next Friday) Did I say this Friday? I meant next Friday.

4. My purse/wallet was stolen and it had two months' rent in it.

5. My aunt Agnes in Texas is:

    - sick and I have to send her money (Monday)

    - dying and I have to send her money (Wednesday)

    - dead and I have to send her money (Friday)

    - having her funeral today, more money (Sunday)

6. My bank screwed up my account again.

7. I'm all out of cheques. But don't worry – I ordered those ones with the scenic background. They're being shipped out from back East.

8. Little Johnny needs braces.

9. I'll give you half now and you can use my damage deposit for the other half.

10. I had it, but I didn't know I had a hole in my jeans pocket.
11. As soon as I sell my car I'll have it for you.
12. Do you really need it now because I just have to get my car fixed so I can get to work, or else how am I going to make money to pay the rent?
13. Didn't I give you two months' rent last month?
14. The stove is broken and I'm not paying until it's fixed. (Note to Landlords: Check the fuses. I've seen them missing just to fake a sick stove.)
15. I'll pay you a full year's rent if you could just wait until the end of the month.
16. My couch is probably worth more than the rent I owe you. Give me $200 and we'll call it square.
17. How about I do all the yard work around here instead?
18. Well, I don't have it, but I'm sure we can work something out. You are flexible, aren't you?
19. You've really come at a bad time.
20. Can you believe I don't remember where I hid the rent money?
21. The people upstairs didn't have to pay their rent at the beginning of last month. How come I have to?
22. You don't believe me. You're calling me a liar. Don't worry, you'll get it. You'll get it soon.
23. I haven't had a chance to get to the bank yet.
24. I'll bet your wife would like a nice piece of jewelry. Come on in. I'll show you what I have.
25. Didn't you get my phone message? I had to spend the rent money to fix the stove. I think you should owe me something for my time. And, no, I don't remember where the receipt for fixing the stove is.
26. My roommate moved out and she's got the other half.

27. Take a look at this car over here. Man, this car is you!
28. Don't worry. I'll pay interest on the late rent. You'll make a profit.
29. My bonds mature at the end of the month.
30. I sold my entire stock portfolio and I should be getting my cheque in the mail any day now.
31. I had to completely clean this entire suite out from top to bottom from the last tenant who was here. That's why you're only getting half the rent.
32. My boss ripped me off and I didn't get paid this month.
33. I'm taking $200 off the rent because the fridge went on the blink and all my food spoiled. I fixed it myself and I'm not charging you, so you're getting the better deal.
34. Come on in and have a beer. I'll tell you about this idea I have.
35. Oh, it's you. I thought it was my friend. I wasn't planning on being home when you got here.
36. Here's a cheque, but don't cash it for a while.
37. Here are two cheques just in case the first one bounces.
38. Why do I always have to pay at the beginning of the month? Can't I wait until the end of the month, and that way I'm paying for the time I've stayed here?
39. I'm not paying all the rent because I think you're charging me too much.
40. If you want the rent that bad, I'll have my biker friends deliver it to your house personally this afternoon.
41. I haven't got my damage deposit back from the last place I rented, so you'll have to wait.
42. My cat/dog/hamster/rat was sick and you wouldn't believe what vets charge these days.
43. My sister from Winnipeg isn't here yet and my lasagna isn't cooked. You'll have to come back another time.

44. As soon as my boyfriend gets back from the racetrack we'll have all the rent.

45. You should have got me before I went to the pub last night.

46. Little dost thou know that the love of money is the root of all evil for all mankind!

47. It's not like you're going to go broke this very second just 'cause I don't have the rent, eh?

48. Like my new pierced tongue and tattoo, man? Cost a bundle.

49. This is like, so Karma, man. We were all just sitting around and talking about this rent thing when all of a sudden you show up. Just can't talk about it, man, 'cause you're weirding me out too much.

50. I needed the money for a deposit on the place I'm moving into at the end of the month.

* * *

I believe the handbook is broken down into four parts. The above is the first part. The second part is made up of variations, twists and combinations of the first part. The third part is a type of diary where they keep score. You know, things like:

- list of excuses and dates that have already been used
- stars beside the most successful excuses
- which appliance was blamed for breaking last time
- what excuses the other tenants are planning on using next month so as not to overlap
- which phase Aunt Agnes is in

There's also a Miscellaneous chapter to record:

- whose turn it is to buy the next vehicle

- your days to phone the Landlord so he gets at least one phone call a day, and who's on the night shift
- brand names of the garbage bags that tear the easiest
- who's on **Landlord Rent Watch Alert** at the beginning of next month
- whose turn is it to perform this month's sacred **Pagan Ritual Tenant Fire Dance** and pass the Landlord voodoo doll to the next in line
- whose turn is it to phone Revenue Canada with this month's top tip
- dates and times for the next secret tenant meeting to discuss future action plans

I believe there are other features in this beautifully hand-crafted, quality handbook. I figure the front cover has tastefully stitched edges with embossed gold foil lettering where the tenant's name is engraved on it. The top left-hand corner probably has the gold emblem of the Tenancy Branch proudly displayed in a hologram. Other features include a secret pouch on the inside of the front cover called *Quel Scandale* where they keep secrets smuggled in by the Underground.

There's probably another section that contains the *Personal Motivation Accessories Fold-out Kit* in case of an emergency. Each page has an inspiring *Quote of the Day* to help motivate tenants through those tough times.

This soft, leather-bound book is sponsored by the Tenancy Branch, so there is no cost to the tenants. I'm sure the book comes complete with a Tenancy Branch team photo with the words "I Guarantee It" scribbled across the bottom. Right next to that is a place to insert the picture for the *Tenant of the Month* award.

This inspirational, built-to-last book also comes complete with a calendar (with the rent days circled in red) and a matching pen and pepper spray set. You will notice the most recent versions of the book have the new *21 Attitude Sampler Set* that has been proven to reduce rent payments.

Now, this is just my best guesstimate of what the book looks like. For all I know, there's some kind of Satanic thing that will prevent me from ever knowing its true appearance. But if any of you tenants ever want to break the Tenant Oath of Allegiance (and probably give up your rights to the Tenancy Branch forever), please send me a copy. I'd love to know how close I was to the real thing.

Oh, I know what you're thinking. Well, Fred...EXCUSE ME, didn't you have scenic cheques that bounced a few times, and didn't you have three cars and weren't you a tenant for thirteen years? Where's YOUR Tenants' Secret Handbook?

Good questions, and don't get your knickers in a twist. This is why I figure there has to be some kind of Supreme Being (how else would you explain beer and pizza ever getting invented?). Bottom line is, I figure Mr. Supreme knew I was scheduled to be a Landlord and the book was withheld. This dovetails right into my Reincarnation Theory (what goes around comes around) where next time around I bet I get a book. (If Mr. Supreme has a sense of humor, he'll probably have me working for Revenue Canada.) Heaven help me if someone's going to make me go through this again!

Oh, by the way, when I finally do leave this Earth I want my full damage deposit back. I always figured that if you leave the Earth (that you have been renting) in good shape, then the damage deposit gets you into the "big suite upstairs." If you don't get your damage deposit back, you get sent back to try again. Three strikes and you're out, meaning you don't get your damage deposit back and you go to the "big suite downstairs," if you get my drift.

Chapter 104

To Whom it May Concern

Dear Tenants: I'm not really a Landlord. It just happened that way. I hate conflicts and I really do like people. I want to make a buck and I understand you don't want to spend a buck. I don't like Revenue Canada and apparently you don't, either. I lose at arbitration, but that's not your fault. I never stood a chance, with you having your own branch bought and paid for. Remember the time you didn't have the rent? Well, Bev, Chris and I still hate you for that.

In the end, it was just one of those biological things. We both needed one another to survive. I hope that some day you become a Landlord. I don't mean that in a vindictive type of way, but I'd like you to see how rosy your world is when you're wearing my glasses. I guess that is being vindictive. Looks like I gained another by-product in my personality from being a Landlord. Thanks a lot.

Dear Revenue Canada: I hope you enjoyed the $50,000 I paid you in Capital Gains tax. I hope you didn't spend it all in one place. It was unfortunate that we didn't get along. I blame it on the language barrier. I speak English and you speak something else.

I wish you well in developing more policies and procedures. Remember, the thicker the better. I believe your idea of cross-referencing unrelated directives to future instructions not yet released should prove interesting for your clients. I know I'm looking forward to many more years of new instructions to decode coming my way.

Dear Banks: How on Earth do you guys manage to make billions of dollars each year? I find it hard to believe you even know where the money is! You're always losing my small amounts of money, so how on Earth do you plan to keep track of a billion dollars?

By the way, I stopped trying to balance my chequebook years ago. When I started getting monthly statements that started off with Page 1 of 8, I just gave up. It seems like half the cheques I deposited got sent back to me anyway, and the way Bev uses ATM machines, you'd think they were slot machines that always paid off. Way too much.

Pop Quiz

Score one right and you can move on to the next chapter. Score all wrong, then return the book. (Apparently, you just don't get it.)

Question 1. Landlords are:
A) Sprayed with the same chemicals used to get rid of Morning Glory.
B) Aliens from a distant planet, but not too distant so that they can send their rent money back home.
C) Stupid people, because if they were smart they wouldn't be Landlords.

Question 2. Tenants are:
A) Responsible for spraying the chemicals on the Landlord.
B) Earthlings responsible for eliminating the Landlord alien race.
C) Smart enough not to be Landlords.

Question 3. Revenue Canada:
A) Taxes the tenant's chemicals.
B) Taxes the Landlord's rent he gets.
C) Collects more taxes from both of the above food groups.
D) All of the above, including taxing anything else that breathes or has breathed in the last seven years.

Question 4. Banks:

A) Will charge you exorbitantly high interest to ensure a fourth-quarter profit margin for their stockholders of one billion dollars.
B) Same as above, but use one trillion dollars instead.
C) Are the real aliens!

Answers:

1(C) 2(C) 3(D) 4(Answer not revealed in case the banks get mad at me and beam me aboard their Mother Ship.)

Chapter 105

Twenty-one of the Most Guarded Secrets of Landlords

These closely guarded secrets are for all the tenants who make our days so extra special. Please raise your left hand, place your right hand on the book and repeat after me. I promise to:
- not abuse this information or update my Tenants' Secret Handbook with it
- only use this information during an emergency equal to, or greater than, a full-scale nuclear attack
- not sell this information to any foreign countries

Okay, go ahead and read them. I trust you now:
1. We do not have a large computer database of personal information, complete with video surveillance cameras trained on each tenant. That's Revenue Canada's job, and they're good at it.
2. We do not have medical, dental, life or disaster insurance to cover tenants. We can barely afford the premiums to cover all the dumb stuff **we** do.
3. We are not blessed with God's speed, nor do we have the patience of a saint. We're old dogs learning new tricks.
4. We do not have all the answers to your problems. We have our pants. We fly by the seat of them.
5. "How To" books are the only books we have time to read. They are our lifelines to survival.
6. The rent we collect is not for us. It's for the banks. They have

all the money, and they're proud of it.
7. Garbage does not magically disappear, nor does it decompose overnight. We haul it away and we hate it.
8. Your car collection in front of the suite does not impress us. We know they don't work, have no value, and we don't want to swap them for this month's rent.
9. We do not love your pets. Sorry to give you the bad news. Break the news to Fifi gently.
10. We know you have a great stereo system. I know it, the other tenants know it, and the neighbors all know it. We know that number ten is not the only volume setting on your system. There are other numbers you can try!
11. We are accountable to a much higher authority for our actions. They're called spouses.
12. Getting us into the "Christmas spirit" should not be confused with a free month's rent in December.
13. We buy light bulbs, fuses, oven cleaners and aspirins in bulk quantities. We also get group rates at the psychiatrist.
14. We like watching horror movies on TV. It is a form of relaxation. It helps put everything into perspective.
15. The School for Landlords does not exist. You can't even buy a book on it. We have no idea how it works. It's trial by fire and water on a daily basis. Give us a break: we're drowning out here!
16. We are not part of any government conspiracy to eliminate affordable housing for you. The government is doing just fine on that project all by itself.
17. The nightmares we have when we're asleep at night are just recaps of the day's events. No offense.
18. When we click our heels three times and repeat "there's no place like home, there's no place like home," we mean it. (Probably because our Huggies are full).

19. We want to give you back your full damage deposit. Keeping your deposit so we can clean your fridge and scrub your toilet is not a get-rich money making scheme.
20. Landlords are not a "species." We're more of a "prototype" until we figure this thing out and get a user manual published.
21. Our motto is and always has been, "Run hard, run scared and don't look back."

So now that you know these Guarded Secrets, let us just summarize by saying, "If you've got a problem, just blame it on the BIG BANG that started the whole evolutionary process, and stop nit-picking on us. We didn't start the thing in the first place, and it's not our fault we're here!"

Thank you for your attention to this matter. This chapter will self-destruct in thirty seconds.

Chapter 106

Life's Good Again

I had come a long way from the Robertson screwdriver era. I actually knew all the names of the tools that I had borrowed. I had put in a sprinkler system that worked, built a pond with three-tier cascading falls, installed a brick patio, and even put in a putting green for Sammy to practice his golf. And I've still got all my fingers and I'm still walking on both feet.

Life is back to a bowl of cherries. When the phone rings, I don't break out in a cold sweat. When someone knocks on the door, I don't hide under the bed. All the people I know are friends. That Fill where "All good things come to those who wait" is kind of true. Although they should really squeeze the word "suffer" in there somewhere to bring it back into reality. I'm down to ten appliances and a couple of water heaters. Still have four lawn mowers and a dozen Weed Whackers that don't work.

As a father, I have to teach mental survival techniques to my son, Sam. Bev would say, "Don't panic, go see Fred." (I think that will be the title of my next book.) Now, it's not like Bev was passing the buck (maybe she was), but what it meant to Sam was that, *If I go see Dad, then the problem just might get solved.* Regardless of what I told Sam, he already was on the road to recovery because he was seeing Dad. It answered the old question, "Who can I turn to?"

I like to walk outside in the yard with Sam when we discuss his "panics." I never dismiss his panics as being trivial because they are real enough to him, six years old or not. But in between the "panic breakdowns," I always point out something like a kayak going by or, "Hey, look at the three swans over there!"

I immediately come back to Sam's problem because I don't try to dismiss it. Eventually the panic breaks down as other things are brought into perspective, and Sam learns where to file the experience in his brain. He realizes life has good things to see and remember, and therefore good things to come. It took me twelve years as a Landlord to figure that out.

After a while, Sam and I are throwing the football and talking about other things we should do some day, and the panic is forgotten. "Hey look, Dad, the geese are up on the lawn again."

"Yup, goose poop happens, Sam." (Or so they say.)

Chapter 107

The Conclusion of the Matter

Well, it's been a year since I sold the fourplex and the duplex. I was out for a walk one day at lunchtime and, as usual during my walks, I gave my brain a chance to run free and do whatever it wanted. Just don't have me walk into a car or telephone pole, I tell it. On this particular day, I took a left instead of a right. I knew this would shorten my one-hour walk by fifteen minutes.

For some reason my brain started to tell me a story about one of my tenants. It was telling the story as if there was an audience listening. I suddenly realized that I had virtually shut out the Landlord experience from my mind, but somehow after a year it was okay to think about it again.

That's when it hit me. More than one person has told me I should write a book. When I got back to the office, I had that fifteen minutes left over from my walk to see if I could put pen to paper. It was a total cleansing. A psychiatrist would have been proud of me. Two months later I finished, and you're holding it. They say that life is just one giant experience, and that there's humor in every situation. It's true, and I feel qualified to attest to that. I hope you enjoyed my life's little experience, because it's all absolutely true.

I also hope you have a wonderful life, because we all deserve one. Oh, and in case you were wondering, my brother Dan, who bought the fourplex with me, is now thirty-three. That's the exact age I was when everything started at the beginning of the book when I was a bachelor and a tenant. Well, Dan and his wonderful wife, Lisa, have two fine-looking boys, and have just about finished building a house on a five-acre property. This house is nothing short of the Taj Mahal. I could fit every tenant and appliance I ever had into his place. He's even putting in a waterfall, just like his dear old brother. Dan's done well for himself.

Now for the REAL conclusion to the matter. Life doesn't just go on. It excels in leaps and bounds while some portions of it do conclude. Landlording concluded for me, and the roses do smell better. I'm afraid goose poop still smells the same, but I just don't run across as much of it anymore. So let's just get straight to the moral issue of the book. It deals with everything you've done up until this point. (You have done *something*, haven't you?)

I've done this, you've done that. I've lived this, you've lived that. I guess I was bad once upon a time, so I got reincarnated as a Landlord for my sins (or possibly bad habits). If you've been bad, you better hope my reincarnation theory is all wrong, or you're soon to be a Landlord, which means I'll be in touch with you someday as soon as I get my copy of the Tenants' Secret Handbook in the mail, plus my case of cheques with scenic backgrounds.

Until then...

Please remember, this book was written for fun and entertainment and was never intended to hurt anyone. OK? No hard feelings, Revenue Canada? Like, you're not going to audit me again, are you?

Fred Miller

Attention

Landlords & Tenants

Do you have a story to tell?
If you do, E-mail me at my WEB site
and you could find your story published in

Landlords II

Please keep your story to under 700 words.
I will ask you for a disclaimer for printing your story,
but I will give you full credit in the book.

Landlord2@home.com

www.ingramcontent.com/pod-product-compliance
Lightning Source LLC
Chambersburg PA
CBHW070641120526
44590CB00013BA/805